101 Testimonies of Hope

Life Stories To Encourage Your Faith In God

Published by Testimonies of Hope Press
PO Box 3951, Rock Island, IL 61204
To order individual copies or bulk copies,
visit: www.testimoniesofhope.org

Library of Congress Cataloging-in Publication Data

ISBN- 13: 978-0-615-93682-6
ISBN- 10: 0-615-93682-2

Cover photo: Lauren Cowart
Design: Ryan Hall and Stecker Graphics

Editors:
Emily Cooper and Argrow "Kit" Evans

101 Testimonies of Hope

Life Stories To Encourage

Your Faith In God

Argrow "Kit" Evans

Hope Writers and Hope Artists

Testimonies of Hope Press

*For anyone who has experienced suffering,
healing, restoration, and hope.*

Hope Table of Contents

Hope

Healing

Prayer

Relationships

Solidarity and Justice

Discipleship

Trust

Our Vision

About the Founder

ACKNOWLEDGEMENTS

I want to express appreciation for the special people who believed in Testimonies of Hope and helped make our community possible. Thank you Jacalyn Barnes for believing in the vision. From the beginning you volunteered your time, skills, and leadership to make Testimonies of Hope possible. You have helped to "birth" a ministry and movement of Hope around the world. You are truly a child of God and a gift from God!

Thank you John Hill and Rose Renie Canlas for sharing your web expertise in the form of ministry as Hope Volunteers. I am grateful for our hard-working co-editor, Emily Cooper. Thank you Ryan Hall for helping to bring our book to life. Thank you Rev. Dr. JoAnne Marie Terrell for so graciously writing the foreword for *101 Testimonies of Hope.*

I am thankful for Rev. Dwight L. Ford, Bobbi Ruffin, Rev. Dorothy Warren, Willie Allison, Roxanne Warren, Michael Warren, Miranda Brown, Ronnie Warren, and Dr. Susan Griffith. Thank you family for your encouragement, resources, and guidance.

Thank you to every Hope Writer, Hope Artist, and Hope Translator who contributed their unique creativity, making *101 Testimonies of Hope: Life Stories to Encourage Your Faith In God* possible:

Rev. Sonsiris Tamayo-DeWitt, Kerri Rigsbee, Bobbi Ruffin, Jessica D. Mason, Author LaShena D. Smith, Iris Ann Agustin-Capus, Sabrina Shelton, Crystal Simmons, Norma

P. Dollaga, Rowena "Apol" Laxamana-Sta. Rosa, Kimberly Annette Hardy, Author Terry-Ann Scott, Niya Tanyi, Georgia Chambers, Adelita V. Maxilom Skrzypek, Ha Feh, Zamansky L. Moore, Rod Spidahl, Andrew Spidahl, Dr. Stephanie Fletcher, Claudia Lizette Aguilar Rubalcava, Segun Olagunju, NaTisha Peacock, Paseka Khosa, Dr. Adrian Manley, Rocky McKoy, Sonya Taly, Nwabisa Tolom, Brian Konkol, Sandhya Rani Jha, Cheryl Ngobeni, Rebecca Holderman, Pastor Dameian Battle, MBA, Ericka S. Dunbar, Debbie Wallace Whittington-Robinson, Erika Lobe, Maggle Chandler, Kent Forbes, Veronica Nikka Bolkeim Teico, Margaret A. Brunson, Junior Versailles, Ebony Holt, Jasmine Joy Landry, Marceline Niwenshuti, Blakely Gooch, Candace Richards, Warrel Stephen Mothoa, Roxanne Van Wyk, Sivu Tywabi, Rose Renie Canlas, Merchades Method Rutechura, Kirk Louis, and Gladson Thomas.

Thank you! Your voice is going to bless thousands; dare I say millions of people around the world. Hope lives in you. Thank you for sharing your *Testimonies of Hope*!

FOREWORD

"Hope" is the thing with feathers -
That perches in the soul -
And sings the tune without the words -
And never stops - at all -

And sweetest - in the Gale - is heard -
And sore must be the storm -
That could abash the little Bird
That kept so many warm -

I've heard it in the chillest land -
And on the strangest Sea -
Yet - never - in Extremity,
It asked a crumb - of me.
Emily Dickinson[1]

I dwell in Possibility –
A fairer House than Prose –
More numerous of Windows –
Superior – for Doors –
Emily Dickinson[2]

Hope may very well be "the thing with feathers," perched within the human soul, that flies, halting or soaring, despite, into, above, and beyond the variable, often enough *extreme* conditions of our lives and times: the withering heat of unrequited love, or of seasonal, or

---

[1] Emily Dickinson (1830-1886), "Hope is the Thing With Feathers," dated circa 1861, first published in 1891. Cited in *Emily Dickinson: 1082 Poems* (www.poemhunter.com), 2012, p. 319.
[2] Emily Dickinson (1830-1886), from "I Dwell in Possibility," dated circa 1862, first published in 1929. Cited in *Emily Dickinson: 1082 Poems* (www.poemhunter.com), 2012, p. 356.

unremitting drought; the frigid cold of uncaring words from a once-warm heart, or of a compromised Earth; the battering winds that threaten our fragile emotional sensibilities, or that destroy, quite literally, whole cities. Yet, to "dwell in Possibility..." One would be hard-pressed to find a better textbook definition of the word "hope," hope that is enfleshed, engaged, endured, and that itself endures, sometimes - perhaps, *often* - beyond a reasonable expectation that one's hope will be fulfilled. Since "faith is the *substance* of things *hoped for,* the *evidence* of things *not seen,*"[3] there is inherent risk in abiding in hope. This is why, in light of the uncertainty of gaining whom or what we desire, those of us who live in hope are often called "dreamers." Yet just as surely as faith and hope (and love, for that matter) involve risk, they also yield the sweet fruit of our imaginings and more. So, as often as we dream, we who live in hope, who "dwell in Possibility," discover ourselves awake, aware, and awash in *limitless possibility,* having deferred to the infinite creativity within and around us, through the exercise of hope. We who dwell in "Possibility" recognize hope as a divine gift that is not merely a buttress to the vagaries of human faith and love but is also an anchor against fickleness, despair, mediocrity, and the mundaneness of our mortal existence.

In Dickinson's ode to her own creative writing process, the poet thus yields to the theologian an empowering insight. She testifies through her art, and I bear witness, that the gift of hope is, like poetry itself, an inexhaustible resource, an invitation to excellence, and a preface to infinite possibility. The bard of scripture wrote, "Hope deferred

---

[3] Hebrews 11:1.

makes the heart sick, but desire fulfilled is a tree of life."[4]
Yet hope by its very nature is always deferred, poised to
wait; situated in the arena of power; empowering, but not
itself fully empowered. The paradox of hope deferred is
the opportunity it affords to those of us who dwell in it to
awaken in others this same belief in infinite possibility.
Indeed, it is our work, to testify to dimensions of
redemption as yet unseen, to testify to the power of a God
who "specializes in things thought impossible," who "can
do what no other power - none but the Holy Ghost power -
can do."[5] This power of Possibility is represented in holy
writ (that is, in Dickinson's art form as well as Christian
scripture) through the liminal symbol of a *Door*. To
Dickinson, poetry relative to prose is "More numerous of
Windows - Superior for Doors," so that deep, solid truth
may be told in its compact lines. In the gospel of John,
Christ Jesus's "I Am"(*"ego emi"*) statements (which imply
his divinity) include his confession, "I Am the Door,"[6] that
is, to new, abundant life. Moreover, the fourth gospel
promises that, "to as many as receive him, to those
believing in his name, [Christ] gives *power [possibility]* to
become the children of God." To abide in hope, to "dwell in
Possibility," is to rest in this promise, childlike, and to trust
this Power, as the 19th-century poet intimates but does not
confess, neither in our stead, nor on our behalf. Rather, she
elicits the confession from our own lips. My testimony is
therefore:

---

[4] Proverbs13:12, New American Standard Bible.
[5] From the gospel song, "God Specializes," written by Gloria Griffin and popularized by the
Roberta Martin Singers (of which Griffin was a member) in many recordings since the 1950s.
[6] John 10:7, 9: "I am the door of the sheep." "I am the door: anyone who enters through me
shall go in and out and find pasture."

"I dwell in Possibility" because God, the Creator of the ends of the universe, is the Source of my life and creativity.

"I dwell in Possibility" because God, the Door allows me access again and again to new life.

"I dwell in Possibility" because God "is able to do exceedingly, abundantly above all I can ask or think."[7]

"I dwell in Possibility" because "with God, nothing shall be impossible."[8]

"I dwell in Possibility" is the testimony of every believer in the Christian story, a fantastic melange of things thought impossible: a Virgin Birth, water-made-wine, miraculous healing, feeding of multitudes, Resurrection. Many people simply cannot affirm the literal truth of these events, which are constantly evoked in the tenets that form the doctrinal basis of our faith and practice. Yet, according to scripture, these "impossible possibilities" are in fact "signs" that point to things we human beings *experience* as even more impossible; namely: the actual forgiveness of sins; our own capacity, both to receive newness of life, abundant life, everlasting life, life "which is life indeed,"[9] and to perceive our worth. And the most impossible possibility of all, without which there is no good news, no source of encouragement, neither for us nor for this world? I believe it is that, dwelling in limitless possibility, abiding in hope, we will most certainly encounter the unfailing

---

[7] Ephesians 3:20: "Now unto him that is able to do exceeding abundantly above all that we ask or think, according to the power that worketh in us."

[8] Luke 1:37: "For with God, nothing shall be impossible."

[9] Cf. I Timothy 6:18-19: "Instruct them to do good, to be rich in good works, to be generous and ready to share, storing up for themselves the treasure of a good foundation for the future, so that they may take hold of that which is life indeed."

grace and unconditional love of God, no matter our extremity. Our personal, emotional vulnerabilities and the predicaments of our age notwithstanding, we need the courage to hope.

St. Paul famously wrote, "And now abide faith, hope, and love, these three; but the greatest of these is love."[10] Yet, of all God's great gifts, hope is the most impeccable. By hope we demonstrate whom and what we love. By hope we remain faithful in the face of the impossible. In this volume, *101 Testimonies of Hope: Life Stories to Encourage Your Faith In God*, fifty-three authors, artists, and awakened dreamers from around the world testify to the power of hope to make impossible possibilities realities in their lives and circumstances. I have written this Foreword in celebration of this ecumenical, intercultural, multilingual demonstration of the efficacy of hope, not merely to produce miracles but also, perhaps fundamentally, to be a sign to the hopeless that God *is*, and that God in our midst is still our Comforter, our Advocate, our Guide; the One who receives us, forgives us, heals us, and ushers us in to new life. I hope these stories will inspire you as they have inspired me.

JoAnne Marie Terrell, PhD
Associate Professor of Ethics, Theology and the Arts
Chicago Theological Seminary

---

[10] I Corinthians 13:13.

INTRODUCTION

I am humbled and overjoyed to introduce you to *101 Testimonies of Hope: Life Stories To Encourage Your Faith In God*. On February 14, 2013 I founded Testimonies of Hope: The Intercultural Christian Devotional Website at www.testimoniesofhope.org. I noticed the need for a safe online community where Christians from different cultures, languages, ages, and ethnicities could come and share their experiences of suffering, healing, and restoration through devotional writing and faith-based art in order to encourage each other. The vision became a reality and our online community continues to grow daily via our website, Facebook, Twitter, and YouTube. God is so good!

We have read about our sisters and brothers healing from leukemia, broken relationships, eating disorders, domestic violence, racism, poverty, injustice, natural disasters, genocide and the list continues. I am amazed at the radical faith that our Hope Writers, Hope Artists, and Hope Translators have and more importantly the radical healing power of our Lord and Savior, Jesus Christ. The Testimonies of Hope community reminds me daily, *"but with God all things are possible." Matthew 19: 26 (KJV)*

101 Testimonies of Hope takes you on an encouraging journey through life stories about Dreams, Faith, Hope, Healing, Prayer, Relationships, Joy, Love, Solidarity and Justice, Discipleship, and Trust. These stories are the testimonies of fifty-three Hope Writers and Hope Artists, shared through their devotionals, poetry, and artwork, assisted by Hope Translators, who also contributed Bible verses in fourteen languages.

Representing twelve countries and fourteen languages, these contributors are all members of the Testimonies of Hope community (www.testimoniesofhope.org), within which testimonies such as these are called Hope Devotions and Hope Artist Reflections. One-hundred percent of the proceeds from this book will go back to our community for Hope Donations to ministries around the world!

Every day our courageous Hope Artists and Hope Writers boldly encourage one another. I pray that as you read these sacred testimonies that you will also be healed, restored, and that unwavering hope and faith in Jesus Christ will be nourished.

"Let us hold fast to the confession of our hope without wavering, for he who has promised is faithful. And let us consider how to provoke one another to love and good deeds, not neglecting to meet together, as is the habit of some, but encouraging one another, and all the more as you see the Day approaching." Hebrews 10: 23-25 (NRSV)

God bless you!

Argrow Kitnequa "Kit" Evans
Founder, Testimonies of Hope:
The Intercultural Christian Devotional Website

We Invite You To Join Testimonies of Hope!
Website: www.testimoniesofhope.org
Facebook: Testimonies of Hope
Twitter: @TestimoniesHope
YouTube: Testimony Hope

The first testimony in this book, **From Posttraumatic Stress Disorder to Testimonies of Hope!** is written by the founder of Testimonies of Hope, Argrow "Kit" Evans.

1. From Posttraumatic Stress Disorder to Testimonies of Hope!

English (Spanish)

I was up late that Tuesday evening. It was around 11:30. I had taken a nap earlier in the evening, so I was now cleaning my kitchen and next I was proceeding to clean my bathroom. I was listening to the latest music my friend from America had sent me. I had been in St. Kitts for almost a year serving with a community development program. I felt like I had a new family and community on this small island in the Caribbean. I was content. It was finally starting to feel like home.

That night when I was in the bathroom getting my cleaning supplies from under the sink I heard a noise at the door. When I went to look the door was cracked open. I closed the door thinking that the wind blew it open because I had a visitor earlier. They must not have shut the door. As soon as I shut the door and I locked it I knew something was wrong. My instincts told me that someone was in the apartment other than me. To this day I still don't realize why I didn't trust my instincts.

I entered the kitchen with my hands up ready to protect myself. Within seconds a man jumped out from behind my kitchen wall. Masked, slanted eyes, hot breath, dark clothes, and a knife that had already started swinging at my hands. He told me to take off my clothes. I changed the subject to money, "You don't want my body, you want money." The next 15 minutes in this real-life horror film would change my life forever. Within that time frame I was strangled, robbed, beat, cut, and there was an attempted rape against my body, mind, and spirit. Unconsciously throughout the entire assault I said, "Jesus, Jesus." He told me to shut up. Unconsciously I started saying, *Psalms 23:1 and Psalm 23:4 "The Lord is my shepherd. I shall not want. Even though I walk down the valley of the shadow of death I will fear no evil; your rod and staff- they comfort me."* He told me to shut up again.

That night, by the grace of God I was able to get away. With a naked body, bloody hands, and a tortured spirit and mind I was able to fight back, break a knife in half, and ask the rapist to use a condom before attempting to rape me. In the midst of all of this, Jesus allowed me to slip underneath the assaulter's grip, crawl to the door, and my neighbors who heard my screams drug me upstairs to "safety." Thank you Jesus!

So how have I healed from this? How have I been restored? It was difficult. I was diagnosed with something called Post Traumatic Stress Disorder. This caused me to have anxiety attacks, sleepless nights, and a fear of knives. Sometimes I could not walk down the street alone or enter a house without checking every room and under every bed. At first I was upset and angry. I went through a trial. They caught the man. I testified and he received 46 years in prison. I still question: is prison really justice?

For a long time I felt sorry for myself. I had to tell my story because I needed people to feel sorry for me. I needed people to know what happened to me, so I shared every chance I could. This provided me with some healing;

however, when I went home I still stared at the door to make sure no one entered while I was sleeping. Over the years, sharing testimony, counseling, dance, plants, friends, family, and love have healed me. Jesus is the one who is continuing to heal me, and he is also restoring me.

In my travels and in ministry I have realized that EVERYONE has a testimony. I have heard about people's suffering all over the world; however, I have also heard about their healing and restoration through their relationship with Jesus Christ.

Everyone has a testimony. Many have been abused, raped, hungry, lonely, sick, neglected, and the list goes on. But, there is something about believing in something beyond ourselves that gives us hope and a peace that surpasses all understanding. *Philippians 4:7 reads: "And the peace of God, which surpasses all understanding, will guard your hearts and your minds in Christ Jesus." (NRSV)*

Please join our online community, Testimonies of Hope: The Intercultural Christian Devotional Website, for daily inspiration. You will be blessed by stories of suffering, healing, and restoration: Testimonies of Hope!

Argrow "Kit" Evans (Rock Island, Illinois, USA)
Founder, Testimonies of Hope:
The Intercultural Christian Devotional Website

Spanish (English)
Filipenses 4:7 dice que "Y la paz de Dios, que sobrepasa todo entendimiento, cuidará sus corazones y sus pensamientos en Cristo Jesús." (NRSV) **Hope Translator: Rebecca Holderman (Centralia, Washington, USA)**

Dreams

2. Hope for Materialized Dreams

English (Afrikaans)

I remember, as early as elementary school, teachers encouraging me to dream. Moving along to secondary school, teachers began telling me ways that I could start working to materialize those dreams.

Occasionally I am surrounded by hopeless people. I often wonder why my sisters and brothers have no hope. Do they not have the power to be resilient? Do they not have the capacity to develop their faith in hopeless situations?

Lately I have been pondering these questions. I wonder if the reason why persons fail to dream beyond what they experience in the now is that our communities aren't communicating and equipping them with the tools to materialize their dreams. Imagine if we told children that they could be nurses, CEOs, and other occupations that require extensive education yet never sent them to school to learn the guidelines of these occupations.

On the one hand, children could possibly dream about these occupational roles because they have interactions with persons in these occupations and society esteems educated people. On the other hand, children could instead take on the mindset, "no one cares about me," and never set out to enter these occupations because we fail to support them.

My hope is that every person will realize his or her value as God's prized humanity. I believe that so many individuals' spirits are damaged by the hierarchical system in society which values individuals at the "top" of the system and devalues nihilism in those at the "bottom." A scripture that I have heard time after time is "love thy neighbor as thyself," yet I rarely see it practiced in society. Instead, those who consider themselves at the top "talk down on" those "below".

There is a song, "Money can't buy me love." While money is a substantial way to provide, I believe that an effective way to help people make their dreams a reality is to provide unconditional love and have conversations with them.

I pray that we reach back to the African proverb, "I am because we are and we are because I am." This proverb promotes kinship. If we are to move beyond hopelessness and unmaterialized dreams, we have to become lovers of souls! We must show our sisters and brothers that their souls matter!

"And the second, like it, is this: 'You shall love your neighbor as yourself.' There is no other commandment greater than these."
Mark 12: 31 (NKJV)

Hope Writer: Ericka S. Dunbar (Atlanta, Georgia, USA)

Afrikaans (English)
"En die twede hiermee gelyk,is dit: Jy moet jou naaste liefhe soos jouself.Daar is geen ander gebod groter as die nie." Markus 12:31 (Die Ganse Heilige Skrif Bible, 1940) **Hope Translator: Roxanne Van Wyk (Durban, South Africa)**

3. Seeing My Destiny in The Stars

English (Malayalam)
"Then he took him outside and said, Look at the sky. Count the stars. Can you do it?" - Genesis 15:5 (MSG)

There's something about stargazing that makes me feel really small, but in a good way. Recently my sister and I went stargazing at a campground outside of Queenstown, New Zealand. This experience happened at a stage in my life in which I have really been growing closer to God, and in which He is constantly imparting wisdom in the most unexpected of places.

Since there isn't much light pollution in New Zealand, the stars are really visible. As always when I look up at the stars, I was captivated by the fact that they appear to be so tiny from our point-of-view, when many stars are actually bigger and brighter than our Sun. This led me to think about how far away stars must be, to look so small, and how bright they must be, to be seen from such a great distance. As I became temporarily lost in my thoughts of and amazement about the vast power, beauty, and quantity of the stars, I began to realize how small my problems are in the grand scheme of life, and in relation to God's plan for me.

Just as God placed a rainbow in the sky to remind us of His promise to never again destroy the Earth with water, I feel that He placed stars in the sky to remind us of His great plan for us – to remind us that this life is bigger than our current, linear situation and to help us see that our destiny is too great and our God too powerful for us to be derailed by the relatively small trials we face on this Earth.

And that's why it's not a negative thing that stars make me feel small; I may be physically tiny on this Earth and in this universe, but I am an important speck on this large canvas of life. I play a part in something much greater than me, and any struggle that I may be going through at the time – financial instability, health issues, a lost loved one – is not big enough to distract me from my destiny. In fact, like Paul in 2 Corinthians 12:9-10, I should revel in these trials, for it is in these times of my own weakness that I am made strong in God.

Did you know that shooting stars happen rather frequently, but that light pollution makes them hard to see? That night, stargazing in Queenstown, I spotted five shooting stars in half an hour! Have you seen any shooting stars lately, or is something polluting your view? Through the stars, God helped me to realize that I can't let the small things distract me from seeing the beauty that is His divine plan for me.

Hope Writer: Niya Tanyi (Los Angeles, California, USA)

Malayalam (English)
"Pinne avan avane purthu kondu chennu: Nee akashathilekku nokkuka; nakshathrangale ennuvan kazhiyumenkil ennuka ennu kalpichu. ninte sandadi engane akum ennu avanodu kalpichu." -
Ulpathy 15:5 **Hope Translator: Gladson Thomas (Kottayam, Kerala, India)**

4. Failure is Nothing to Fear

English (Sepedi)
If one were to conduct a survey to learn the most common

human fears, it is safe to conclude that failure would be near the top of the list. Due in part to the high value our society places upon success and achievement, we recognize through the twists and turns of life that everyone has – in some shape or form – firsthand experience of the fear of failure.

We often fret over falling short, we frequently agonize about disappointment, and we even lose sleep from the thought of letting others down. With such thoughts in mind, it is important to reflect upon the all too common fear of failure, for such fears can be devastating and debilitating if left ignored or unresolved.

While the fear of failure has many sources and consequences, as people of faith we recognize that Jesus sets us free from the fear of failure and offers the freedom to embrace life in its fullness. While the various societal pressures around us can be cruel and unforgiving, in the eyes of Jesus we are received as we are and fully included as members of God's all-encompassing community. While these beliefs do not eliminate the pain that moments of failure can bring, the reception of God's love provides us with a larger-picture perspective and longer-term strength to see moments of failure as a small part of God's grand narrative, and in turn we can learn from our various mistakes and move forward with renewed wisdom and guidance.

All together, while we make numerous missteps with each passing day, we need not be afraid of failure, for Jesus does not require perfection, and we can be free to move forward from fear to faith to action through the abiding presence of God. We can take risks, step outside of our

comfort zones, and embrace all that God is calling us to be and follow where Jesus is leading us to go.

In other words, while our imperfections are exposed each day, through Jesus we are made complete, and while the journey of life may be bumpy, the destination of our existence is full of peace and joy. And so, we can be honest about our various shortcomings, but we can also receive freedom through the forgiveness of God, and in response to this unconditional acceptance, we may continue to reflect God's love through peace, love, and abundant grace for the glory of God and sake of the world.

"I am content with weaknesses, insults, hardships, persecutions, and calamities for the sake of Christ; for when I am weak, then I am strong." -2 Corinthians 12:10 (ESV)

Hope Writer: Brian Konkol (Saint Peter, Minnesota, USA)

Sepedi (English)
Ke ka moo ke teeletjego ka mafokodi, mahlapa, maima, dihlomaro le ditlaeishego ka baka la Kriste, gobane ge ke fokola ke mo ke nago le maatla. -2 Bakorinte 12:10 (ESV) **Hope Translator: Warrel Stephen Mothoa (Soweto, South Africa)**

5. Follow Your Dreams

English (Spanish)
"Now glory be to God, who by his mighty power at work within us is able to do far more than we would ever dare to ask or even dream of—infinitely beyond our highest prayers, desires, thoughts, or hopes." Ephesians 3:20 (TLB)

When your dream comes from God, it will be so massive in your life that you cannot do it on your own. If you could do it on your own, then you would not need faith.

The dream that you have – the idea, the concept, the very thing that you have been thinking about doing that would be of real benefit to other people – where do you really think that idea came from? God will never tell you to do something that contradicts His truth. A dream is a vision, a goal, a desire – these are all things most of us know we need when we are working towards success.

Dreams are the goals and visions that fire your heart and saturate your soul. They are those continuing visions of what you want your life to be at its highest level of fulfillment. Dreams are what you want to do, how you want to do it and what kind of person you want to become in the process.

Your destiny and reason for living are wrapped up tightly in your dreams – they are similar to the genetic information inside of a seed. The dream in your heart contains your spiritual "DNA" – the blueprint for who you really are. Your dream is that vision for your life that continuously burns on the inside of you that cannot be ignored. Your dream will keep coming back to your mind because it is part of who you really are; it will never leave you until it becomes your manifested reality. A dream is like a magnet that pulls you toward itself.

I do not believe that there is a man or woman without a dream, because God designed each and every member of the human race to have dreams. When people do not recognize the dream that God has placed in them, they will become totally frustrated in the present and will miss their future and the expected end for their life.

Please be totally aware that your dream did not originate with you. It resides within you, because God put it there. He is the source of your dream. When people dream without God, they find it unsatisfying. Every person must come to Jesus for his or her dream to make sense. When your dream is God's dream, it is totally unstoppable.

Hope Writer: Author LaShena D. Smith (Atlanta, Georgia, USA)

Spanish (English)
"*Y a aquel que es poderoso para hacer todo mucho más abundantemente de lo que pedimos o entendemos, según el poder que obra en nosotros.*" *Efesios 3:20* **Hope Translator: Rebecca Holderman (Centralia, Washington, USA**)

6. Preparing to Fly

English (Spanish)
One change that I see in myself that's increasing more and more every day is my faith and strength in God! With such a busy schedule and with dealing with school, church, and family I find myself weak and worn at times. Then I turn to Jesus and I think about all the times that God has been my very best friend when my earthly friends have let me down and I think about how he's healed me and brought me out – and that's enough for me to feel my help coming! Before I know it, I have not only a testimony but also a shout! Like my dad says "When praises go up, blessings come down!"

There's a scripture that I turn to constantly: *"But they that wait upon the Lord shall renew their strength; they shall mount up with wings as eagles; they shall run, and not be weary; and they shall walk, and not faint." Isaiah 40:31 (KJV)*

Whenever you feel down and need hope, turn to this scripture, and I promise that in no time you will have renewed strength!

Hope Writer: Kerri Rigsbee (Kannapolis, North Carolina, USA)

Spanish (English)
"Pero los que confían en el Señor renovarán sus fuerzas; volarán como las águilas: correrán y no se fatigarán, caminarán y no se cansarán." -Isaías 40:31 **Hope Translator: Rebecca Holderman (Centralia, Washington, USA)**

7. Coming Out

English (Haitian Creole)
For those of us finding our way onto a spirited walk with God, we reach a time when the material world no longer satisfies us.

A time when rhythm and reason tell us that there is something more to this life.

Something deeper. Something fuller. Something that is separate and altogether holy. Something that only God can give us.

Ashamed and humbled, carrying the heavy burden of our

carnal ways, we are ready to be set free.

Ready to be claimed. Made separate. Redeemed and restored.

And in this wake, this realization, we come out.

Out of Babylon. Out of the ways of this world. Out of the grips of the deceiver.

Our eyes are opened. Our paths cleared. Our mouths silenced.

We flee. Finding our substance, our rest, and our place in the arms of Our Savior.

We find in Him awe. We find in Him grace. We find in Him the substance of things not seen.

Most importantly, we find Him. In His Majesty. In His Glory. In His Might.

We find a life-giving and intimate relationship.

A promise, fulfilled. A tear, dissolved. A cry, rejoicing.
We find God.

"Go ye forth of Babylon, flee ye from the Chaldeans, with a voice of singing declare ye, tell this, utter it even to the end of the earth; say ye, The Lord hath redeemed his servant Jacob." Isaiah 48:20 (KJV)

We praise you O Heavenly Father. We lift up your name

for you are great and mighty. We worship you at your feet. Praise your glorious name.

Hope Writer: Jasmine Joy Landry (High Rolls, New Mexico, USA)

Haitian Creole (English)
"Ale non! Peyi Babilòn lan, nou lakay moun Kalde yo kouri, ak yon vwa nan nou deklare chante, di sa a, absoli li menm nan fen a ak latè a, pou nou di, Mèt la ki delivre Izrayèl, sèvitè l 'yo."
Isaiah 48:20 (KJV) **Hope Translator: Kirk Louis (Midwest City, Oklahoma, USA)**

8. Hope Artist Reflection: "Free"

English (French)
Hope Artist: Rocky McKoy
Location: District Heights, Maryland, USA
Poem Weblink : http://vimeo.com/rockabye/free

FREE - a Poem by Rocky McKoy

What is the name of this piece of artwork?
"Free"

What inspired you to create this piece of art?
I was feeling down. I prayed and heard "write." With most of my poems I simply write and don't allow the pen to leave the paper until whatever is in my mind has made it onto the canvas. I wanted to get out of my current state of mind.

I believe there is more to living than just a mundane existence of going to work and coming home. I can inspire, create and be fruitful in some form of an idea that God has planted in me. I want to live out the dreams God has placed in me.

With this particular piece I knew I had to do more than just write it, it had to be seen. So I asked my wife to read it because I felt the voice of the poem was not mine, but that of a woman wanting to get out of her past and live in the present.

How do you see hope within your artwork?
I want people to know "you are not your past." Your past does not define you or "who you BE in God." We are a culmination of our choices. Freedom comes when we decide we are tired of where we are and take the action to do something different in order to take hold of a better future.

What is one Christian scripture that is connected to your art?
"Surely your goodness and faithfulness will PURSUE me all my days, and I will LIVE in the Lord's house for the rest of my

LIFE." Psalm 23:6 (NET)

How do religion and culture influence your work?
God speaks to me through spoken word and visual artistry (film and paintings). These art forms are the tools I use to express how I think. Culture changes so much as far with technology and ways of expressing one's self. I find it interesting to see how people are telling their stories through graphic art and video editing; It pushes me to see what God has put in me and how I can show it to others.

French (English)
"Certes, ta bonté et ta fidélité me poursuivra toutes mes jours,Si la bonté et la fidélité de Dieu sont à ma poursuite, alors pourquoi suis-je courir de Dieu?" Psaume 23:6 (NET) **Hope Translator: Andrew Spidahl (Holland, Michigan, USA)**

9. Hoping for Healthy and Holistic Relationships Between Women

English (Afrikaans)
Browsing through greeting cards, I picked up one created for Hallmark's Mahogany line. This card used the Adinkra symbol of West Africa to represent love, devotion, and loyalty – virtues that are part of the relationships that Black women share together.

Friendships are the ties that bind us, the strength that holds us, and the spirit that sustains us woman-to-woman, sister-to-sister. I was excited to see a symbol that promotes togetherness, commitment, support and community.

Growing up, I was very shy and withdrawn. In my times

of separation and isolation, I began to watch people, studying relationships and interactions. At an early age, I noticed the dynamics of broken relationships between females – mothers separated from daughters, sisters at odds, broken friendships, estranged relationships between females in books and films. I even noticed female biblical characters at odds with each other, even given the minimal presence of women in the bible.

It seems that there has been a conspiracy to shatter the spirits of women – to dismember our souls and dismantle our minds because we possess a giftedness that renders us intelligent, proficient, free, strong, substantial, beautiful, resilient, wise, and so much more.

Recipients of degradation, deprivation, humiliation, dilapidation, confrontation, mortification, shame and disgrace, we were, and sometimes continue to be, presented in society as null and void, unacceptable, useless, worthless, voiceless, void of mental capacity, lacking social ability, unimportant, and insignificant, used only for sexual gratification.

Our powerful wombs have been abused, disrespected, neglected after males drink their fill, even mutilated, objectified and commodified – those same wells deep enough to plunge in for pleasure and good enough to bring forth the very essence of life, that is, all generations to follow.

Female genital mutilation is practiced all over the world. Yet it is not only our genitalia that have been mutilated but also our very souls. Our souls have been maimed, damaged, disfigured, and scarred in the name of power, authority and domination. We are the victims of a patriarchal nation. Victims of hatred, shaming, blaming, and defaming, some women have internalized the negativity and have perpetuated it through committing woman-on-woman crime, speaking death-sentencing words and judgments, or offering no balm to heal the many wounded souls! How many people hear the cries to halt the offenses against innocent women simply trying to live?

This greeting card symbol gives hope that there are women who will not stop working for justice, for peace, for help, and for relief against hatred and disdain. We wave this symbol proclaiming we will love, we will have devotion, we will be loyal, we will remain and sustain! My hope is that all women across race, ethnic and color lines together will stand in solidarity to fight with enduring strength for respect, mutuality and generosity.

My hope is in the willingness of individuals to counter the death-sentencing stereotypes proclaimed over girls and women worldwide. My hope is in the wisdom of the matron sisters who don't mind encouraging, and giving constructive criticism. My hope is in the smiles of the sisters who are genuinely happy to see other sisters thrive and be elevated. My hope is in the spirit of interdependence within the lives of sisters who recognize that we are not alone and can accomplish more together than we can individually.

My hope, sisters and brothers, is in the love that we house in our hearts, which has power to overcome obstacles that would prevent us from living in love with each other. This is my testimony of hope!

"I praise you because I am fearfully and wonderfully made; your works are wonderful, I know that full well." Psalm 139:14 (NIV)

Hope Writer: Ericka S. Dunbar (Atlanta, Georgia, USA)

Afrikaans (English)
"Ek loof U,omdat ek so vreeslik wonderlik is;wonderlik is U werke! En my siel weet dit alte goed." -Psalm 139:14 (Die Ganse Heilige Skrif Bible, 1940) **Hope Translator: Roxanne Van Wyk (Durban, South Africa)**

Faith

10. God Can Do A Miracle

English (German)
Today happened.

For many, many weeks I had great pain in my legs and upper arms. To get dressed or to stand up was very painful. I could walk, but running was impossible.

That condition came upon me suddenly, and I thought it was a kind of flu. I thought I could just wait to be healthy again. But I got worse and the pain in my legs and arms increased more and more. Even my prayers seemed to go unanswered.

So I went to the doctor. Even then I couldn't get a good diagnosis, because one blood test result was missed. The doctor advised me to take painkillers for the weekend. First I was disappointed, but then I remembered I had pain medication at home and did not need to buy it.

I took one pill and prayed. After a while the pain lessened and I could start to move my legs and arms nearly normal again.

Then I got a biblical picture in my mind:

"Having said this, he spit on the ground, made some mud with the saliva, and put it on the man's eyes. 'Go,' he told him, 'wash in the Pool of Siloam ' (this word means Sent). So the man went and washed, and came home seeing." John 9: 6-7 (NIV)

God's way is not our way, perhaps not the way we would like to see, but it can be the vision we receive in our heart.

God can do a "miracle" in any case.

God is no robot or automation. It is important to listen, to be patient, to trust, to love, to forgive, and not to give up.

Everything we do we should do for God's honor, praise and glory, and we should thank him.

Hope Writer: Ha Feh (Kiel, Germany)

German (English)
"Als er dies gesagt hatte, spuckte er auf die Erde; dann machte er mit dem Speichel einen Teig, strich ihn dem Blinden auf die Augenund sagte zu ihm: Geh und wasch dich in dem Teich Schiloach! Schiloach heißt übersetzt: Der Gesandte. Der Mann ging fort und wusch sich. Und als er zurückkam, konnte er sehen." John 9, 6-7 **Hope Translator: Ha Feh (Kiel, Germany)**

11. Cosmos

English (Spanish)
The cosmos – How can one write about that which is unfathomable? How can I describe what is indescribable? Immeasurable and unquantifiable?

The cosmos can be seen in all existence. Yet, it chooses to also live in our mere human existence. Going from beings of the universe to an incarnate existence. Teilhard de Chardin puts it this way: "A spiritual being having a human experience."

The innumerous and ancient giants surround the earth,

curious about our life experience and when I lived among them we gather around the light of the moon. My mission, if I choose to accept it, was to put on flesh and learn about human acceptance, human condition.

The cosmos – How can one write about that which is unfathomable? How can I describe what is indescribable? Immeasurable and unquantifiable?

I cannot explain what is too vast. To speak about God is a human fabrication. God is beyond words – too slow and yet too fast. Beyond imagination. And still we must try to quench the thirst, through artistic channeling and metaphor fabrications – to give God personification and earthly representation.

There is a force behind evolution – a plan to save the earth. To save us from danger and learn about human behavior: its destructive nature – the chaos, confusion, and its sickening hatred.

There is a force behind evolution. Creating and fueling revolutions, heeding the wild call of Sophia – so we can save the biosphere from the sins of greed, lust, gluttony, wrath, envy, pride, and sloth.

The cosmos – How can one write about that which is unfathomable? How can I describe what is indescribable? Immeasurable and unquantifiable?

Keen observations, self-awareness, and meditations – brings us just a bit closer to the outer and inner illuminations. Making us less of a poser, bringing cessation of eternal frustrations and vexations.

Swimming in the luminous darkness of the cosmos – I am

learning, we are learning the cosmic flow. The body is an instrument, and we need to pay attention to it – for the cosmos speak through it.

The cosmos – How can one write about that which is unfathomable? How can I describe what is indescribable? Immeasurable and unquantifiable?

"For ever since the world was created, people have seen the earth and sky. Through everything God made, they can clearly see his invisible qualities – his eternal power and divine nature." - *Romans 1: 20 (NLT)*

Hope Writer: Rev. Sonsiris Tamayo-DeWitt (Hayward, California, USA)

Spanish (English)
"Porque desde la creación del mundo, sus atributos invisibles, su eterno poder y divinidad, se han visto con toda claridad, siendo entendidos por medio de lo creado, de manera que no tienen excusa." -*Romanos 1:20 (NLT)* **Hope Translator: Rebecca Holderman (Centralia, Washington, USA)**

12. A Nightmare to Speaking With Faith

English (Swahili)
On February 6, 2010 I turned 27 years old and had a big party! I had the works – food, family, and friends. After a while we said our good byes.

During this time I was a student at Belmont Abbey College, but what people didn't know was that I was tired. I wasn't eating correctly, and every day I went to school with no energy – plus I had people in my circle that were really stressing me out.

On February 8, 2010 my mother thought that it was best to see a doctor about my energy level. We went to the hospital. What started as a routine appointment ended up being a nightmare. I was admitted, and an I.V. was put in so that platelets could be given. I endured an eye and bone marrow biopsy. Keep in mind it's still the same day. By the time I was moved to a hospital room I didn't really know if I was even alive. Once I woke up, my mom, brothers, and sister were around looking concerned.

Finally Tuesday came, then Wednesday. On Wednesday three doctors entered my room and a second I.V. was put in. I was told that I needed surgery on my stomach the next day. I said okay to the surgery, and I had my mother call my family. One thing about my family is that they stick with me, and when I call they come. I wanted them to be the last people I saw before surgery.

Right before they arrived I remembered that I hadn't looked at myself. So I got out of bed and looked in the mirror. I cried at my sight because I couldn't recognize myself. The eye biopsy had turned part of my face another color.

Listening to my family talk I felt strength that I could do all things with God, remembering the exact scripture that my mother had given me as a child in the hospital. *"I can do all things through Christ who strengthens me." - Philippians 4:13 (NKJV)*

Right after the family's visit, my doctor came in and canceled my surgery. Instantly I went from being a believer to speaking the truth because my words the night before to my mom were revealing themselves. My words to her were "Ma, if I need surgery I will be fine, because I know that God will take care of me. He said that he won't put more on me than I can bear – right? So I'll be fine!" I spoke with faith and authority.

I believed with my whole heart, and my mom stopped crying because she believed too. I've been praising my God ever since. It's easy to say the words "I believe" but to say those words with conviction brings power you could never imagine.

I thank God for being a constant friend that never let me down! God healed me and was there for me and I know that he will be there for all his children who believe in him, and who speak with faith!

Hope Writer: Kerri Rigsbee (Kannapolis, North Carolina, USA)

Swahili (English)
"Naweza kufanya mambo yote katika yeye anitiaye nguvu."
Wafilipi 4:13 (NKJV) **Hope Translator: Merchades Method Rutechura (Dar es Salaam, Tanzania, East Africa)**

13. Let Faith Do Its Job!

English (Sepedi)
On January 2, 2013, I received a text from my sister saying that my grandmother was being rushed to the hospital. I panicked, because my grandmother means the world to me. I panicked also because it's late at night, I am five

hours away in another state, and I have a class in the morning – which happens to be a J-term class so it's abbreviated and if I leave town now I will have to drop the class, which means I can't graduate in May.

After what seemed like hours of holding my breath, I learned nearly five hours later that my grandmother was being placed in the ICU. I decided to exhale, releasing all fears about my grandmother's health to God's care.

As I rewind, I need to say that my grandmother had known a little over a year now that she had kidney failure. Afraid to go on dialysis because she didn't want to spend the rest of her life suffering, she stalled, praying for a miracle from God.

We spoke about the possibility of a kidney transplant, me willing to give her one of mine in hopes of buying a little more time. We had completed the paperwork to see if she was eligible for a transplant just the month before. Her body grew fatigued and then weary as she was now in the hospital, unable to breathe with high blood pressure. I was stuck in another state, praying, "God please don't take my heartbeat away."

I was asking, "How can this be? A woman who has reflected the life and ministry of Jesus who bore the cross on Calvary?" My grandmother not only took care of her children, but took in seven grandchildren and took care of countless others, sacrificing her time, finances, literally everything she had. "Lord, will you forsake her, too?" I asked, thinking about the question that rang from Jesus' mouth. "Why won't you give me the permission to leave and go be with my grandmother, God? I am not willing to forsake her but I don't want to disobey you either." So, days later, I heard the words, "without faith, it's impossible to please God."

Oftentimes, we think that we have to have our hands on every thing. I felt horrible that I could not be physically present. But God taught me in this experience that my faith manifested into a spiritual presence that brought comfort to my grandmother, peace to myself and pride to God. Instead of putting my hands on it, I had to put my mouth on it through prayer and allow faith to do its job. Many things I hoped for have materialized – and my grandmother is still living!

"Now faith is the substance of things hoped for, the evidence of things not seen." Hebrews 11:1 (KJV)

Ericka donated a kidney to her grandmother and had a successful transplant on Dec 10, 2013.

Hope Writer: Ericka S. Dunbar (Atlanta, Georgia, USA)

Sepedi (English)
"Tumelo ke bonnete bja tše re holofelago gore di tla hlaga, ke go kgolwa tše re sa di bonego" *Baheberu 11:1 (KJV)* **Hope Translator: Warrel Stephen Mothoa (Soweto, South Africa)**

14. Even When I Am Faithless, He is So Abundantly Faithful

English (Spanish)
In late 2007 I was working for a phenomenal non-profit in

DC, experiencing the most fulfilling time of my career. Unfortunately, funding issues arose, and I was let go in September. I was crushed! My faith was bruised and so was my confidence.

After four months back home in Delaware, my brother challenged me: "you don't belong here in Delaware; there's a bigger dream for you." So at Christmas I said a prayer and committed to moving back to DC. The last paycheck I received I gave away to a friend in need, testing my belief that, ultimately, God would meet my needs. I was now penniless.

I began sending and posting resumes like crazy. I sent a detailed email to friends describing the kind of job I believed I should have, but nothing happened.

On Martin Luther King, Jr. weekend in 2008, I packed my bags and headed down to DC to volunteer for a conference. I could stay at my cousin's house while looking for jobs. A job expo fell through. I told myself to just find a job at a restaurant and I turned in applications at Clyde's and at Ruby Tuesday, but neither was ready to hire. As I was about to get back on the metro, defeated, someone thrust a flyer into my hand: Potbelly's was having a job fair.

I walked in and had two interviews in rapid succession. There were three stores looking for openings, one right next door to the bank where I used to work. I prayed, "Lord, any store but that one," but, of course, that one wanted me the most. I was anxious about running into my former co-workers from the bank, but my soul was humbled with gratitude and I accepted the job offer. To eat

I needed a job, and this one would feed me every time I worked. (The provision of my Lord is thorough.)

Eventually I worked the heavy lunch shift and a few of my former co-workers did come in. They didn't react at all with the sort of shock that I had been fearing. I remember praying, "Lord I can handle anyone but Bee," the guy who knew what everyone else was doing. Sure enough, about three weeks into my "career" at Potbelly's, in walked Bee. Boy, I wanted to pull my hat down over my face and bolt right into the back, but I knew I would surely get fired for that. So I prayed, "Lord, give me the strength." I served Bee and thanked him for his business. That was much easier than I had feared.

Three days later, a phone call came in at my job. I picked up the phone, an old friend and bank colleague said, "Segun, I heard from Bee that you are working at Potbelly's." She had just gotten an email from Jackie making a last ditch effort to locate me and she wanted to put Jackie on the phone for a three-way conversation. Huh! Jackie came on and said, "Segun, I've been trying to find you for the last two months to recommend you for working for me." My jaw dropped open.

While I was still wrestling through the process of humility in the search for a job, providence had already ordained it that someone was looking trying to give me a job! This was now late February, so that meant that in late December God had already been working this out for my good. Coincidence maybe, but I prefer to call it providence!

Even while I am faithless He is so abundantly faithful. Soli deo gloria.

"I will sing of the loving kindness of Jehovah for ever: With my mouth will I make known thy faithfulness to all generations." Psalm 89:1 (ASV)

Hope Writer: Segun Olagunju (Johannesburg, South Africa)

Spanish (English)
"Por siempre cantaré de las misericordias del Senor: con mi boca daré a conocer tu fidelidad a todas las generaciones." Salmos 89:1 **Hope Translator: Rebecca Holderman (Centralia, Washington, USA)**

15. I Have Decided to Follow Jesus!

English (Haitian Creole)
I grew up in a family that went to church, prayed, knew and feared God. But the question is, "Did I?" I went to church all right; I knew the best and comfortable part of the church to get a seat; I knew where I was not allowed to go and where I was allowed; I knew the pastor and the elders of the church (even their seats in church) and I assure you I could tell pretty well when we had visitors; I knew the lead singers in the worship team and what kind of songs they were more likely to lead. But for many years I failed to know the reason behind going to church and behind the lead singers singing (although I enjoyed it, and probably that's why I kept going).

This is what happens when the gospel is according to whoever is at the top of your playlist, and the media has become your bible, searching scriptures of magazines to be told you are something you are not. I thought going to church made me righteous: one of those situations when you think going to church is like going to Kauai, if you buy smoothies for about 5 times you get the 6th one free. I thought the number of times I went to church would allow me access to heaven.

I needed an intervention. Christ came into my life one Sunday when I allowed Him to, and He came to do a last provision, which reminded me that on the cross he was fully extended. And me? I was given an extension, hear me an extension and on that day I knew that *"He must become greater, I must become less."* John 3:30 (NIV) Knowing very well that one day we all are going to be audited, I had to stop adjusting the scriptures so they could best fit me.

I had to stop pretending and had to fully surrender my life. This has been the best decision I have ever made. So I have decided to follow Jesus, I see the cross before me and I ain't turning back!

Hope Writer: Cheryl Ngobeni (Giyani, South Africa)

Haitian Creole (English)
"Li fèt pou li vin pi gran, mwen dwe vin pi piti." Jan 3:30 (NIV) **Hope Translator: Kirk Louis (Midwest City, Oklahoma, USA)**

16. The Reality of Faith

English (Sepedi)
My twin nephews are going home today! It is a momentous occasion in the life of my family. Twenty-six days ago, Ethan and Isaac were born. They were born

premature and spent most of the past month in the neonatal intensive care unit trying to regulate their temperatures and gain weight. And, today, they are finally both going home with mom and dad. We are all so grateful they are healthy and that they are here!

You see, Ethan and Isaac's story does not just go back 26 days; it is a story many years in the making. My brother has wanted to have children for as long as I can remember. It took some time to get settled, but the story about how my brother and his wife came together is a beautiful testimony to God's grace in each of their lives (and all of ours!) They were both very excited to get started having a family.

When they began trying to get pregnant, they had some difficulties but did not worry too much. They got checked out by the doctor. Then, there was a procedure. And another procedure. And many promises by doctors that each procedure was sure to work. For a long time, my brother and sister-in-law maintained faith that God would work out this situation. Through several years of emotional roller coasters, they also sometimes struggled to keep that faith.

I admire my brother and sister-in-law a lot. What inspires me so much about their story is how real they have been throughout. Sometimes I could tell there was much pain in the waiting and in the lack of answers. Other times they seemed settled, yet hopeful. Other times one could sense anger. Yet through all seven years, they gave themselves permission to be honest with themselves, with God and with each other. I have found their example of faith to be very liberating for me. I think it takes trust in a God who really cares, and faith in the strength of your relationship to be that vulnerable. It takes courage to offer your true self and to wrestle deeply and honestly.

As this new family finally arrives home, we remember and honor the journey that has brought them. I cannot claim that God especially favored my brother and his wife because of their faith. There are too many faithful couples for whom the results are different. But we recognize the miracles that my nephews are – as every child is. And truthfully, this auntie has been tearful and rejoicing all day. But it is not only because I am grateful for these beautiful children; I am also so grateful that God allows us to be human. That God understands our suffering and confusion. That God actually desires us to be real with who we are, what we feel, and that Jesus identifies with us in exactly that place. God is in the midst of it even when it is hard to see.

"Through Christ you have come to trust in God. And you have placed your faith and hope in God because he raised Christ from the dead and gave him great glory." 1 Peter 1: 21 (NLT)

Hope Writer: Maggie Chandler (Atlanta, Georgia, USA)

Sepedi (English)
"Ka kriste le kgonne go tshepela go Modimo. Gape le beile tumelo le tshepo tša lena go Modimo gobane O tsošitše Kriste bahung A mo nea le letago le legolo." 1 Petrose 1:21 (NLT)
Hope Translator: Warrel Stephen Mothoa (Soweto, South Africa)

17. Packing For Purpose: No Excess Baggage

English (Spanish)

It was a hectic evening. I'd gotten a call around 5 that evening from my travel coordinator that my flight for Rio de Janeiro would be leaving at 9:05 PM. Mind you, I was almost an hour from my apartment and had absolutely nothing packed, so the pressure was intense. I raced home, threw the necessary items in my luggage and sped down the freeway toward George Bush Intercontinental Airport. Though many don't like the hustle and bustle, I actually find it to be a natural aspect of my life.

After checking in, I picked up a turkey and provolone sandwich from a coffee shop near the terminal and soon after boarded my flight. Now, for some well-needed rest and relaxation while the plane filled. As I unwrapped my sandwich and began to chew, I commenced taking in my surroundings. People were putting their bags in the overhead compartments... some rather sizeable, some compact. I watched as some simply tucked a tiny duffel away while some others wrestled with bulky, heavy, and often, multiple bags, frustrated that they would not fit properly. It was very interesting to watch. Some bags wouldn't fit, so they were forced to place them underneath the seat in front of them, restricting legroom and causing a significant amount of discomfort.

All of this activity reminded me of life. We are all on a journey. But often, we tend to "carry on" things that we don't necessarily need. We accumulate hurt and unforgiveness, unnecessary responsibilities, the consequences of bad choices, and we lug it with us everywhere we go, right along with the agony, discomfort and inconvenience associated with it. Some of us were hurt in our childhood, but we refuse to let it go. We have debts that need to be paid, sickness in our bodies, familial issues, we battle with what we want verses what God wants for us, and it creates weighty baggage. The worrying, doubting, and fear are heavy loads that you weren't meant to bear.

Remember, a lighter vessel travels faster and much more efficiently. It's time we open up those bags and do some sifting, discarding and deleting. Choose to carry on the things that help to assist you rather than weigh you down. Everything and everyone isn't meant to go the distance with you. I remember in church growing up, the old folks would call God a "Heavy Load Sharer." Trust Him today with those things that you need to release. He's waiting, willing and adept!
Blessings and Favor.

"Therefore, since we are surrounded by such a huge crowd of witnesses to the life of faith, let us strip off every weight that slows us down, especially the sin that so easily trips us up. And let us run with endurance the race God has set before us."
Hebrews 12:1 (NLT)

Hope Writer: Zamansky L. Moore (Houston, Texas, USA)

Spanish (English)
"Por tanto, puesto que tenemos en derredor nuestro tan gran nube de testigos, despojémonos también de todo peso y del pecado que tan fácilmente nos envuelve, y corramos con paciencia la carrera que tenemos por delante." Hebreos 12:1 **Hope Translator: Rebecca Holderman (Centralia, Washington, USA)**

18. Hope Artist Reflection: On My Own

English (Filipino)
Name: Bobbi Ruffin
Location: Mebane, North Carolina, USA
Artwork: "On My Own"- Bobbi Ruffin and Savvi
Song Weblink:
http://www.youtube.com/watch?v=0shYIvKrLWU

What is the name of this piece of artwork?
"On My Own"

What inspired you to create this piece of art?
Both Savvi and I are advocates for positive urban music.
More specifically, we love to make music that empowers

young women to be themselves. This was truly the inspiration behind "On My Own".

How do you see hope within your artwork?
With this song, I see hope on multiple levels. First, the collaboration of myself and Savvi speaks on its own because we are two different ethnicities coming together for common goals- to uplift others. Next, I see hope in this song because it's a message to other young people to accept who they are and all that they can be in life without worrying about what other people think about them. Being an individual includes not being ashamed about who you are, what you've done, and the things you like. This song is encouragement to any listener to do just that.

What is one Christian scripture that is connected to your art?
"What shall we then say to these things? If God be for us, who can be against us?" Romans 8: 31 (KJV)

How do religion and culture influence your work?
The above scripture is actually a lyric in my verse. When I wrote this song, I thought about day-to-day living and all the things that have the potential to take away our joy. One of those things is the perception of other people toward you. When we are constantly consumed by what other people think about us, we cannot focus on who we truly are... who God says we are. Once we reach a point to where we are 100% dedicated to God's will and what He says about our lives, other peoples' thoughts about us should not matter. My belief in God and my passion for urban art fuels everything I create. It is my hope that through the arts, others will be encouraged and empowered to let their own light shine each and everyday!

Filipino (English)

"Ano ang ating sasabihin sa mga bagay na ito? Kung ang Dios ay kakampi natin, sino ang laban sa atin? " Mga TagaRoma 8: 31* **Hope Translator: Rose Renie Canlas (Baguio City, Philippines)**

19. A Test of My Faith

English (Spanish)

Have you ever endured something twice? The whole time you feel confused and wonder why it seems like God keeps testing you with the same thing more than once – whether it's being patient, forgiving, near the end of a huge accomplishment, or showing love towards an enemy.

You ask yourself, "God, why am I going through this again?" When we ask for patience God doesn't zap us with patience. He puts us in situations where we can grow, and he eventually shows us the very thing that we've been praying for.

A dove and the color blue for me are the symbol and color of hope and peace. When I look at the image of a dove I can't help but to think about the story of Noah and Jonah. They both ran and didn't want to do what God commanded them to do. With God they faced the incomprehensible and after the test a newfound overwhelming peace entered their being.

I believe that we're tried more than once for two reasons: one, there was something we didn't learn from the first experience and, two, God is testing us to see if we have really received the very thing that we've been praying for and if we are applying that in situations in our own lives. Some people think we test God, but sometimes God will test us as well.

When you see yourself in a situation like I listed above use this scripture for encouragement. I often have and it's helped me to get through. *"The Lord is my portion, says my living being; therefore will I hope in Him and wait expectantly for Him."* Lamentations 3: 24 (AMP)

Hope Writer: Kerri Rigsbee (Kannapolis, North Carolina, USA)

Spanish (English)
"El Señor es mi porción, dice mi vida; por eso en él espero y espera con expectación la llegada de él." Lamentaciones 3:24 *(AMP)* **Hope Translator: Rebecca Holderman (Centralia, Washington, USA)**

Hope

20. "My Psalm of 23"

English (Afrikaans)
"Lord," I prayed, "what is this Lord? Please, help me."
Like never before in my life, God seemed so distant, silent.
For my previous 22 years, He had spoken peace over me in
the middle of the night. At the age of 23, was I too old to be
his baby girl? "Lord please," I cried silently. After seeing
three different doctors during that spring, I finally had a
name for my sleepless nights, racing suicidal thoughts, and
consuming fear. Bipolar... mental illness... but, I thought,
isn't that for... other people...

A few months after my diagnosis, I found myself talking to
God: "Father, is this what you've thought of me my whole
life – just damaged goods?" The relief of being able to
sleep at night with the new medication was dampened by
the fact that I had gained nearly 30 pounds in just a few
months. The medications caused extreme weight gain,
increasing the risks of diabetes and death – not to mention
that these meds cost $400.00 a month, unimaginable for a
graduate student's budget. "Lord, who is going to love me
– fat and crazy?" "Oh, Lord," I said, as tears rolled down
my face night after night.

Through this time, I doubted God's love for me. Fighting
bitterness, I arrogantly demanded to know why I was sent
this storm. I prayed feverishly throughout the day. I read
my Bible compulsively before bed. I attended worship
services twice on Sundays, women's Bible study on
Tuesday night, trying to prove to God that I was worthy of
His love. "Lord, please; Lord, please" I cried at night. He
seemed silent.

But... during those dark, sleepless nights, when tears flowed down my eyes, staining my Bible and soaking my pillows, God's word was slowly seeping into my heart. Though I am still being treated for bipolar disorder, the healing of my heart came from the truth of God's word. I know now that God, through Christ, whispered, "My grace is enough for you, Kimberly. For My strength and power are made perfect and show themselves most effective in weakness."

Through my Psalm of 23 I learned that God will never leave you nor forsake you. Believer, you may be going through your Psalm of 23, your Psalm of 33 or of 43 – or maybe you are a seasoned saint in your Psalm of 63, 73, or 103. Hold on, knowing that God's grace is sufficient. It's enough.

"For the LORD God is a sun and shield; the LORD bestows favor and honor; no good thing does he withhold from those whose walk is blameless."Psalm 84: 11 (NIV)

Hope Writer: Kimberly Annette Hardy (Baton Rouge, Louisianna, USA)

Afrikaans (English)
"Want die Here, God,is 'n son en skild,die Here sal genade en eer gee; Hy sal die goeie nie onthou aan die wat in opregtheid wandel nie." Psalm 84:11 (Die Ganse Heilige Skrif Bible, 1940)
Hope Translator: Roxanne Van Wyk (Durban, South Africa)

21. Hope Artist Reflection: "Hope Unseen"

English (French)
Hope Artist: Erika Lobe
Location: Baltimore, Maryland, USA

What is the name of this piece of artwork?
"Hope Unseen"

What inspired you to create this piece of art?
I'm going to be honest and tell my true inspiration for this piece. I have a ritual with a great friend of mine that when we get together, which ends up being about twice a year, we always try to do some type of craft. We have kind of exhausted all the mainstream crafts such as painting and gingerbread houses, so I was searching for something a little more creative. I took to Pinterest in search of something to inspire us. I came across string art and from there I realized that the possibilities are endless!

How do you see hope within your artwork?
My portrayal of hope is a little more obvious. When it

comes to art, I am a firm believer of expressing creativity, but also allowing room for individual interpretation. Despite that, sometimes it is nice to have a daily reminder that is simple and to the point. You don't have to think, just read and appreciate. With this piece in particular, I made use of the negative space. In this case, when you see the word "hope," you are observing the void left by the extraneous elements. It's a little reminder that... well I will leave the interpretation up to you!

What is one Christian scripture that is connected to your art?

"So we do not lose heart. Though our outer self is wasting away, our inner self is being renewed day by day. For this light momentary affliction is preparing for us an eternal weight of glory beyond all comparison, as we look not to the things that are seen but to the things that are unseen. For the things that are seen are transient, but the things that are unseen are eternal." 2 Corinthians 4:16-18 (ESV)

How do religion and culture influence your work?

I am very fortunate to have traveled to several places outside of the United States. Along the way, I have seen many different styles of art. While in Malawi, I was impressed by the methods of creating recycled glass beads. While in Ghana, I was captivated by the artists ability to take old tin cans and make them into musical instruments. In Benin, I befriended a painter in the village next to mine. He had no training, but he painted the most beautiful scenes of everyday life in Africa. Each of my pieces are inherently influenced by the things that I see and feel. I think that it is pretty hard to suppress your experiences from making an appearance in your art.

I can't leave out the fact that my mother is an artist. She always encourages me to try new forms of media. It certainly helps to have people around who are supportive of your artistic expression. Nobody said I have to be a professional artist, so for me, it is all about personal expression. When it comes to art and creativity, it seems innately unavoidable that your sentiments and experiences will wind up in your creation, and that is a beautiful thing!

French (English)
"Donc, nous ne perdons pas courage. Bien que notre couche extérieure s'en aille en ruine, notre moi se renouvelle de jour en jour. Pour ces afflictions du moment se prépare pour nous un poids éternel de gloire au-delà de toute comparaison, que nous ne regardons pas aux choses visibles, mais aux choses qui sont invisibles. Pour les choses qui se voient sont transitoires, mais les choses qui sont invisibles sont éternelles." 2 Corinthiens 4:16-18 (ESV) **Hope Translator: Erika Lobe (Baltimore, Maryland, USA)**

22. My Story: Immigrating from the Marshall Islands to Hawaii

English (Marshallese)
Aloha my brothers and sisters!

I want to share my testimony with all my friends and family out there to get them to know my life and also my Heavenly Father and his son Jesus Christ, who loves us. I want to thank him for all the great things that he has blessed me with. I am so grateful to take this opportunity to share with the world.

Argrow "Kit" Evans

My name is Veronica Nikka Bolkeim Teico. I was born on December 22, 1976 in Ebeye, Marshall Islands. I am the daughter of Nerrow As Dana Bolkeim. I have four siblings and am married to Romeo Teico. We have a son named Donny T. Lucky.

I am a citizen of the Republic of the Marshall Islands. I moved to Maui, Hawaii in 2002 and I have been living in Maui for 11 years.

I remember when I first came to Hawaii in 1998 with my parents, younger brother, and uncle. On our way here, on the airplane, they passed out the immigration forms to fill out. We couldn't understand any of it. I could read in English, but I couldn't understand what we read. Although I couldn't understand, I tried my very best to fill out the immigration form.

That was my first time on a new island that didn't speak my language, Marshallese, but only English. Even though it was difficult to speak or understand, I really tried. It was really hard for my family and me to speak the language. I did not really know how to speak English, but I knew that I was strong.

Later, I was able to take my Marshallese friend and family to their doctor who spoke English. I talked for them and helped them fill out their forms. I also drove them where they had to go.

Today, years later, I am an interpreter in many ways. I am involved with Faith Action for Community Equity (FACE) – Maui Community, and I enjoy what I am doing. I have learned so many new things. I am so happy to work with people because without them I haven't done anything. I learn from them and I am grateful for what I do for a living.

My favorite scripture is: "In the beginning was the Word, and the Word was with God, and the Word was God." John 1: 1 (ESV)

This is the first Scripture I heard from the Holy Bible and it helped me to remember that there is a God who loves us!

Hope Writer: Veronica Nikka Bolkeim Teico (Marshall Islands)

Marshallese (English)
"Ilo jinoin Nan eo, im Nan iben Anij , im Nan Anij." John 1: 1 (ESV) **Hope Translator: Veronica Nikka Bolkeim Teico (Marshall Islands)**

23. Hope Artist Reflection: Prison or Classroom

English (Jamaican Patois)
Hope Artist: Junior Versailles
Location: Sandy Point, Saint Kitts

What is the name of this piece of artwork?
"Prison or Classroom"

What inspired you to create this piece of art?
A childhood friend of mine was in prison thinking that his life was over. My words of strength to him helped turn his prison experience into a reflecting time. Don't hate the darkness, learn to close your eyes and see clear.

How do you see hope within your artwork?
If one of my pieces inspires anyone in making them smile, then my work as an artist is done.

What is one Christian scripture that is connected to your art?

"The reward for humility and fear of the Lord is riches and honor and life ." Proverbs 22:4 (ESV)

How do religion and culture influence your work?
Religion and culture is who I am on the inside, therefore it comes through my art work!

Jamaican Patois (English)
"The reward wey yu get wen yu humble yuself and fear de Lawd, a nuff riches, nuff respec' and you wi live lang." Proverbs 22:4 (ESV) **Hope Translator: Dr. Stephanie Fletcher (Sydney, New South Wales, Australia)**

24. Hope Artist Reflection: The Sun Also Rises

English (Swahili)
Hope Artist: Rod Spidahl
Location: Fergus Falls, Minnesota, USA

On the two of us
gathered, solemn
this day's sun also rises.

Brave sentinel form,
catching with me
these early rays.
Simple tulip-life
Rising undaunted
from grasslands untended.

Someone planted you,

life happened-
Left and abandoned

Friendly bloom, you
Reflections in white
on the disconsolate.

My arms grasp air
Rooted you push
Up-greening joy!

Haloed moon, staring
Out of cirrostratus
Ice-crystalled-soul

Thin air and cold
Shivering past
Cobweb clothing

Thoughts trapped
beneath the warmth.
brain-heart in fog

Weightier sheets
than tons of droplets
hung in morning blues
Persistent Spirit
draw me to color
in darkened humus

Night-shrouds can
instantaneously wear
First-Morning Gold!

Chaotic ghost-shades
Pray, go beyond Sunday-
"Holy Death is Life Rising, again!"

What is the name of this piece of artwork?
"The Sun Also Rises"

What inspired you to create this piece of art?
The real and deep loss I have felt when a close friend, for whatever reason, moves on, leaving pain in the heart and vacuum in the soul. Too often, as a Christian, I may gloss over the pain and hurt to please other friends or, as I might think, please God. I write both to heal and to help others express pain and loss. Our real humanity: Jesus, as 100% human and 100% divine, is something our Western Christianity needs to re-discover, again and again.

How do you see hope within your artwork?
God's amazing Creation never "forgets" to preach to me, daily, that life is a whole package: we can't know life healing without truly embracing our own darkness and pain; dark gives way to light; winter to spring; cold soil to blossoming color, daily experiences of death and dying to daily renewal of life and hope. This is real hope. Hope for the daily grind of life.

What is one Christian scripture that is connected to your art?
"You have taken my companions and loved ones from me; the darkness is my closest friend." Psalm 88:18 (NIV)

How do religion and culture influence your work?
Karl Barth has spoken about our misinformed conceptions as Christians of God giving us life "directly". Actually,

God in Christ gives us death-to-life as a package. When we "expect" God to give us life directly and not mediate it through the cross, we are asking for a false god–a theology of "glory" that wants nothing to do with the way of the cross. Both are together, inseparable. Our culture often tries to hide the aged, the dying, the hurting from our sight. Christians do not do God a favor when we use our "religion" to live in "La-la land" or deny pain. Real Jesus-life is through pain and self-dying, "though you walk through the valley of death, I am with you!"

Swahili (English)
"Umewachukua wanipendao na marafiki zangu, giza ndilo rafiki yangu wa karibu." Zaburi 88:18 (NIV) **Hope Translator: Merchades Method Rutechura (Dar es Salaam, Tanzania, East Africa)**

25. My Help Comes from the Ceiling

English (Malayalam)
Okay, I know that's not exactly right, but there were many days that I felt like the Lord was in my ceiling. You see, there have been days on my journey when I didn't feel like getting out of the bed. Perhaps you can relate? But, it was as if my entire life was going completely wrong and not according to my plan.

I didn't have a job to get up and rush off to, so I figured there was no use in waking up early just to sit around or have nothing meaningful to do. On those days, I'd wake up, lie in bed until 10 AM and look up at the ceiling. Every depressing thought that I could think would then consume my mind for what seemed like hours (although really more like 30 minutes or so). I'd think about how many jobs I'd applied for the previous week with no return calls, or how my bills were continuing to add up but my bank account didn't match, or how lonely or embarrassed I felt after my divorce.

Eventually, however, I'd remember one simple fact (as I continued to look up at the ceiling) and say to myself, "Margaret, God loves you and God has a plan for your life." I remembered that just like the psalmist wrote in Psalm 121: 2, "my help comes from the Lord" and like God's promise in Jeremiah 29:11 "to prosper me" and "give me hope and a future." I remembered that God has a purpose and plan for everything that I was currently facing, and would face in the future.

Even though I'm not still in that desolate and lonely place, I continue to remind myself that, no matter how difficult the journey becomes, I must remember where my help comes from. And it's a little easier to remember because now I'm reminded of how God provided me with opportunities to use my gifts and skills to earn enough money to pay my bills during a two year period of unemployment. I'm reminded of how God surrounded me with friends who encouraged me and kept me company during a difficult time in my life.

Now, realizing where my help comes from means believing that if God allowed it, then God will help me through it. God's plans and ways and thoughts are so unlike mine (and yours) and learning to trust God with our lives means trusting Him to lay out a plan for our lives. There are times when I just want to react to life's circumstances and make quick decisions. However, through my tests and experiences, I've learned to wait until I find purpose. It is through purpose that God reveals my next steps. It is when I'm able to see the magnificence of God working through what seems to be the craziest experience that I'm able to receive God's help. Even if it means staring at the ceiling.

"My help comes from the LORD, Who made heaven and earth."
Psalm 121:2 (NKJV)

Hope Writer: Margaret A. Brunson (Raleigh, North Carolina, USA)

Malayalam (English)
"Ente sahayam akashatheyum bhumiyeyum undakkiya Yehovayenkil ninnu varunnu." *Sangeerthanangal 121:2 (NKJV)*
Hope Translator: Gladson Thomas (Kottayam, Kerala, India)

26. Hope Artist Reflection: Total Piece of Peace

English (French)
Hope Artist: Erika Lobe
Location: Baltimore, Maryland, USA

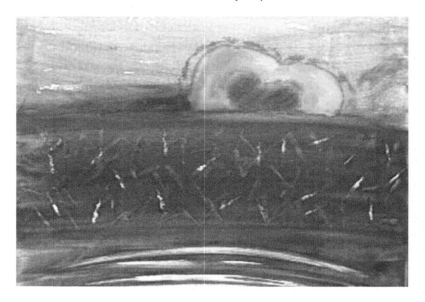

What is the name of this piece of artwork?
"Total Piece of Peace"

What inspired you to create this piece of art?
I created this piece of art on a rainy day with one of my best friends. It was a lovely summer rain, which was calming and so peaceful that it inspired this painting. I began with a heart at the center and it began forming into the numerous elements making up the whole.

How do you see hope within your artwork?
This painting has a little bit of everything, hence the name "Total Piece of Peace". There is a version of the sun and the moon, land, water, and you can find other elements within as well. All the elements come together to form something beautiful and something that evokes a happy feeling.

What is one Christian scripture that is connected to your art?

"You will go out in joy and be led forth in peace; the mountains and hills will burst into song before you, and all the trees of the field will clap their hands." Isaiah 55:12 (NIV)

How do religion and culture influence your work?

Each of my pieces are influenced by the things that I see and feel. This includes religion and cultural influences. These experiences inherently make appearances in my art.

French (English)

"Vous sortirez dans la joie et vous serez conduits en paix; les montagnes et les collines aurez fait irruption dans vous, et tous les arbres des champs battront des mains." Isaiah 55:12 (NIV)
Hope Translator: Erika Lobe (Baltimore, Maryland, USA)

27. Healing Through Forgiveness

English (Jamaican Patois)

When I found out that my boyfriend was using me and exploiting me, I was completely devastated. I just could not believe that someone I loved could hurt me so bad. The pain I felt from his betrayal was indescribable. It was like blood was gushing from a wound in my heart. Bitterness and resentment soon came knocking and I was tempted to retaliate negatively.

I am not sure how I found the strength to pray, but I just kept hearing the words in my spirit; "Guard your heart! Guard your heart!" One day as I prayed and asked the Lord to heal my pain, I suddenly felt like asking myself, "If this was your friend hurting and coming to you for advice, what would you say to her right now?" Right away, there was only one answer I could think of: "Forgive him!" I knew in my heart that the antidote to my pain was forgiveness.

Forgiveness has the power to: (1) deliver you from the negative energy of bitterness and resentment, (2) put you in the place where you can receive God's blessings, (3) eradicate fear and build faith, and (4) distinguishes the humble and pure in spirit from the proud.

The power of forgiveness cannot be overstated. Making a conscious decision to forgive someone who hurt and humiliated me was like an injection of very strong medicine. The road to my healing and deliverance began the moment I decided to forgive.

Have you been hurt, injured, lied upon, cheated, accused, maligned, abused by friend or foe? Paul said, *"Clothe yourselves with compassion, kindness, humility, gentleness and patience. Bear with each other and forgive whatever grievances you may have against one another. Forgive as the Lord forgave you. And over all these virtues put on love, which binds them all together in perfect unity." Colossians 3:12-14 (NIV)*

Forgiveness is effective in any circumstance, relationship or issue. It sets both you and the offender free, takes the weapon out of Satan's hands and nullifies his darts, opens the door for God to take control of the situation, and bring healing. Take the antidote of forgiveness today.

Hope Writer: Dr. Stephanie Fletcher (Sydney, New South Wales, Australia)

Jamaican Patois (English)

"Yu haffi cova up yuself inna compasshan, kineniss, 'umility, genkleness an payshens. Yes man, yu fi tek time wid oneanneder and figive all a de sinting dem weh unnu have 'genst oneanneder. Yu haffi figive oneanneder same way lakka how de Lawd figive yu. An yu haffi put luv pon tap a all a dem good things deh, cause love a de rope weh fi tie up all a dem things deh togedder inna unity." Colossians 3:12-14 (NIV) **Hope Translator: Dr. Stephanie Fletcher (Sydney, New South Wales, Australia)**

28. The Art of Forgiveness

Filipino (English)

Forgiveness is a lesson that has its own rewards, even though it can be difficult to forgive. I offer some support using scriptures to help you in your Christian walk with God. I admit this is a lesson that I struggle with daily because sometimes I don't understand how I can forgive another person, when this person intentionally meant me harm.

I find that holding resentment can be the most poisonous venom to your body, mind, and spirit. It literally causes stress and health problems. Forgiving just so happens to be something that we all must do daily. The bible says in Matthew 18:21-22 to forgive 70X7 which equals 490. The Bible also says, *"Be kind to one another, tenderhearted, forgiving one another, just as God in Christ forgave you."* Ephesians 4: 32 (NKJV)

God forgave us when He died for our sins, and, if we don't forgive each other while on this earth, then we will be judged when we meet Him.

In addition, I've heard several testimonies to how people have found healing & closure in forgiving someone who hurt them or tried to hurt them. God is a good God who made the ultimate sacrifice for us; let us repay Him by living by the word of God! Forgive!

Hope Writer: Kerri Rigsbee (Kannapolis, North Carolina, USA)

Filipino (English)
"At magmagandang-loob kayo sa isa't isa, mga mahabagin, na mangagpatawaran kayo sa isa't isa, gaya naman ng pagpapatawad sa inyo ng Dios kay Cristo." Mga Taga-Efeso 4: 32 **Hope Translator: Rose Renie Canlas (Baguio City, Phillipines)**

29. Whitney Houston: Rest In Forgiveness

English (Afrikaans)
August 9, 2013, Whitney Houston would have celebrated her fiftieth birthday! But, instead of celebrating, the world was commemorating the beautiful Whitney a year and a half following her tragic and sorrowful death. Many, like myself, were still in a state of shock and disbelief – as her future seemed promising and she was definitely endowed with gifts that apparently only heaven could manufacture.

Many have visited Whitney's grave because of her celebrity status alone; the reason for my visit was quite different. I had followed Whitney's career since elementary school, when "The Greatest Love of All," highlighting values of self-love and self-encouragement became a theme song for my school. We were taught: "I am somebody! I am responsible for my behavior, the results of my behaviors and what I become in life" and "Learning is essential and I can do anything I put my mind to because my mind is a pearl." For me, Whitney became the role model for "being somebody" and "doing anything you put your mind to."

As I grew, I realized that Whitney, although a role model, was not quite the exemplary behavior model. I realized that Whitney's behaviors didn't exhibit self-love and that drugs were a major distraction. Though Whitney made choices and experienced consequences, seemingly she lacked persons in her life bold enough to hold her accountable and stand on the front line as drugs waged war against her.

So, my visit to the cemetery was not to celebrate her celebrity or to mourn the loss of a pop star/icon, but, rather, to apologize for being a part of a society and world that failed her... a society that idly sat by and watched her shrink until the point of her demise.

Day to day, we look at community members, our brothers and sisters who have been seduced by drugs and in turn prostitute their souls. They are hungering and thirsting for "righteousness" (not perfection) but for justice, morality and decency by larger society, snorting emptiness and sipping nothingness as they search for a fix that might help them escape the harsh realities of life. Many sit by and proclaim, "What a shame! What a waste! She/he's gonna have to hit rock bottom before..." With every fatal and killing utterance that we breathe, we fail to be our sisters and brother's keeper! We speak death-sentencing decrees over their lives.

What lies within us that we can sit by and watch our sisters and brothers die a sluggish, excruciating, and throbbing death? Is it fear? Lack of faith? Unforgiveness? Lack of compassion? Fear of rejection? If we as humans have been created in the image of God and there are those whose images have been distorted or have gone unrecognized, is it not our responsibility as the offspring of God to hold up a mirror and restore vision to the unsighted?

A wound covered with love, grace, mercy and goodness heals faster than a wound covered with condemnation and judgment. When we engage in the struggle with, and lend support to, those who face challenges, our support becomes therapeutic, curative, restorative, health-giving and life-giving!

We no longer have Whitney to celebrate but we can honor her by honoring those in our communities who struggle with drugs/substance abuse/addiction. We can honor them by showing them that we love them as we love ourselves, by teaching them to love themselves, and by restoring their sight so that they can experience a renewed sense of being!

Rest in Forgiveness Whitney! And may we focus on the conditions of a person's soul rather than on their celebrity.

"Now we look inside, and what we see is that anyone united with the Messiah gets a fresh start, is created new. The old life is gone; a new life burgeons! Look at it!" 2 Corinthians 5:17 (MSG)

Hope Writer: Ericka S. Dunbar (Atlanta, Georgia, USA)

Afrikaans (English)

"Daarom as iemand in Christus is, is hy 'n nuwe skepsel, die ou dinge het verbygegaan kyk, dit het alles nuut geword." 2 *Korinthiers 5:17 (Die Ganse Heilige Skrif Bible, 1940)* **Hope Translator: Roxanne Van Wyk (Durban, South Africa)**

Healing

30. The Lord Offers Hope and Healing in the Midst of Heartache and Suffering

English (French)

The Lord offers hope and healing in the midst of heartaches and suffering. Losing my parents and three siblings at the young age of 8 in the 1994 Rwandan genocide gave me a big shock and then my own denial of this loss for a long time.

I very often missed my mother and the little sister that I used to spend most of my time with at home, before they passed. However, it was only seventeen years later, when I was engaged in research about the role of the Church in the genocide that the pain came to me as fresh as it could be. I went through an emotional breakdown throughout this research. Tears would role on my face while I read for this research. At times, I felt that I had lost any purpose for doing anything, even for living.

In the midst of this, my Christian faith came to my mind. My memory recalled my mother, who was a devoted Christian, gathering us to tell Bible stories. We all enjoyed those moments.

Despite what happens in the world, including the civil war that took away the people I love, God is different from that, I was assured. According to 1 John 4:8, God is love. In addition, I was helped by the readings in my theological study to discover through the life and death of Jesus how God loves peace and justice amongst the people he created.

I saw God in some people who were kind to me. I talked to

one lecturer about my pain, and she lent me her ears to listen. And this helped. I knew that, although bad things happen, God is good and he is alive. I could witness that his goodness can shine through some people. Brothers and sisters in Christ in the church I attended were kind to me. My aunt, who is close to me, gave me a sense of care from a family member.

It became my desire that what happened to me would not cause me to be bitter and to lose hope, but to allow God to shine his love and goodness through me. This is what gave me hope.

No matter what happens, God is and will always be love, such a comforting assurance. We can be God's instruments to give hope. Through every act of kindness we do for another (no matter how small it is and even if it is just a simple smile) we are giving hope.

"Whoever does not love does not know God, for God is love." *1 John 4:8 (NRSV)*

Hope Writer: Marceline Niwenshuti (Pietermaritzburg, South Africa)

French (English)
"Celui qui n'aime pas ne connaît pas Dieu, car Dieu est amour." *1 Jean 4:08 (NRSV)* **Hope Translator: Erika Lobe (Baltimore, Maryland, USA)**

31. Still Dancing

English (French)
I have been dancing for as long as I can remember. Up to this very moment I still dance. Back in 2009, when I was a high school student, I was chosen to represent my school at the annual Rotary Club of Liamuiga dance competition. Needless to say, I was pretty nervous. From the moment I began preparing for the competition to that very night, I prayed. I asked God to give me strength, courage and the will to win.

The night finally arrived, and I was a nervous wreck. It was time for my performance. I did a contemporary piece to the popular song "You Raised Me Up." I felt confident. My presentation was going quite well. Then, suddenly, a loud thump echoed in the room. It was me. I had fallen hard out of a hand stand and unto my back. Quickly, I gathered myself and completed my piece like nothing had happened.

When I got off stage I lay flat on the floor and tears trickled down my cheeks. I could feel immense amounts of pain flow up and down my back. My instructor, along with other persons back stage, tended to me by heating and icing my back. As I lay there I thought for sure I had lost. Moments later, it was time for the winners to be announced. The second place was now being announced. Then it was first place. When I heard my name I was so ecstatic. God had helped me win that night.

As weeks progressed, the pain in my back worsened. I was taken by my parents to see multiple doctors and a chiropractor. I gained temporary relief. I was also told that

I should stop dancing. I thought to myself, how do they expect me to give up this thing that makes me so happy? This is my God-given talent. I then made my decision not to stop dancing.

As I get older I am proud to say I am still dancing! In spite of the back pains, I still glorify God with my talent. Also, I choose to use my gift to encourage others and give hope.

"Heal me, O LORD, and I will be healed; save me and I will be saved, for you are the one I praise."
Jeremiah 17:14 (NIV)

Hope Writer: Candace Richards (Sandy Point, Saint Kitts)

French (English)
"Guéris-moi, Seigneur, et je serai guéri; me sauver et je serai sauvé, car vous êtes celui que je fais l'éloge." *Jérémie 17:14 (NIV)* **Hope Translator: Erika Lobe (Baltimore, Maryland, USA)**

32. Because I Was Addicted, and You Loved and Healed Me

English (Malayalam)
I've been pastoring in a small, diverse, inclusive, kind congregation in Oakland, California for years, and I am proud of the journey we've been on and who we are. On a really good day, my congregation reminds me a little of the clearest glimpse I've ever seen of the church Jesus would join if he were in human form today.

I spent a summer in Kolkata, India when I was 27, mostly to learn my father's native language. I worked at a health clinic for people living with HIV and AIDS, called the Calcutta Samaritans (now Emmanuel Ministries). The program had been started by a passionate Christian couple, the Pavamani's.

When I arrived, I saw the church Jesus intended for us to build: it was made up of the same mixture of people as the clients at Calcutta Samaritans, but they were not just homeless kids, sex workers, and struggling slum-dwellers. They were also leaders, evangelists, and generous hosts. I sang "There Is a Balm in Gilead" and explained the genre of Negro spirituals as songs of Jesus' literal liberating power. That experience would have been enough to make me proud of and content with my new community.

But then I met what the church is really about. One of the men saw me walking and asked where I was going. "Back to Behala," I responded. "The Sunday buses have a different schedule; let me go with you," he offered kindly. He was a clean-cut, middle class man, so I asked how he came to be a part of that particular worship; had he grown up a Christian? "No. I was an addict," he said.

In Kolkata, talking about issues like addiction is not socially acceptable. So his candor was surprising. He shared with me that when he met Vijayan Pavamani, he was completely in the thrall of addiction. And Rev. Pavamani did not judge or impose religion. The man was sent to a treatment center away from Kolkata and rebuilt his strength and healed from his addiction. And in the process he began to wonder about the Christ that the people helping him believed in and asked to learn more.

He found strength to stay clean and sober through the message he found there.

He found and celebrated salvation alongside sex workers, people living with AIDS, and homeless children. So he had dedicated his life to sharing that salvation and love with anyone who needed it. The church at its best is not focused on the right formula or language or dress, but we are focused on saving lives, which is how our own lives are saved.

I met salvation in that little congregation of people the world had rejected in Kolkata ten years ago. And when I witness it in my own congregation, I think, "this is where Jesus would hang out." And I am grateful.

"Therefore he is able to save completely those who come to God through him, because he always lives to intercede for them." Hebrews 7:25 (NIV)

Hope Writer: Sandhya Rani Jha (Oakland, California, USA)

Malayalam (English)
"Athukondu than mukhantharamai Daivathodu adukkunnavarkku vendi paksha vadham cheyan sadha jeevikkunnavanakayal avare poornamai rakshikkuvan avan prapthanakunnu." -Ebrayer 7:25 (NIV) **Hope Translator: Gladson Thomas (Kottayam, Kerala, India)**

33. So He Meant It That by His Stripes We Are Healed

English (Xitsonga)
This is a piece about my mother; her name is Phyllis.

So it started small, "just a little cough and she will be all right the next morning", because that's how it usually is. But see, we don't live a life of "because it happened this way yesterday, it's sure going to happen the same way tomorrow" – unpredictable, that's what it is. We refused to ask God what was happening because we thought the Doctors had it all under control and Oooohhh they had it under control all right. They made it worse by giving her the wrong dose, and in our heads we never knew that it was a "wrong" dose for His appearance in her life.

See, God reigns supreme in situations where we can never predict His presence. I felt like the devil had beaten me down. I wasn't even sure in what state of mind I was in. My thought process became a huge plate of complexities while I ran haphazardly in the dark due to fear; a fear of losing what meant so much to me. And then I heard Peter in the book of Romans say: *"I reckon that the sufferings of this present time are not worthy to be compared with the glory which shall be revealed to us-ward. "* Romans 8:18 (ASV)

In that moment I paused, tried to talk to God about it, but every time I tried to say something I always got a knot in my throat and couldn't say a word. Before I knew it, my tears spoke words that my mouth couldn't verbalize. All I could ask was "Why is this happening?"

I started looking at other people's lives and wished I were them. One thing I had to learn is that we people are different and our differences are not a reason to be jealous, but instead are God's fingerprints. At that minute, when I thought I was okay, I remembered this one night when my phone rang. It was my mother calling; I was scared to answer because something inside of me told me it was bad news. For a few minutes I was hung up on "why me?" I was hung up on "why my mother?" because she had suffered enough. I was hung up on "why was our faith being tested for this long?" But see, God was hung up for my sin. And before He was hung up, He was beaten, He was bruised, and He was wounded for us. So I told myself, "Enough with my hang -ups because His hang-up reigns supreme."

I finally answered the phone, and my mother told me she was in the hospital. This time I refused to go down on my stomach but did go down on my knees. There was not one tear running down my cheeks. I declared and I declared even more: *"But he was wounded for our transgressions, he was bruised for our iniquities; the chastisement of our peace was upon him; and with his stripes we are healed."* Isaiah 53:5 (ASV)

Now I know that He meant it. If they ask you who said it, you can tell them: "Cheryl." And if they still can't comprehend, then they can go to the Father and get it from Him, because my mother is now fully healed!

Hope Writer: Cheryl Ngobeni (Giyani, South Africa)

Xitsonga (English)
"A soriwa, a tshikiwa hi vanhu,munhu wa mahlomulo,la tivaka maxangu, la soriweke tanihi xilo lexi yilaka,kutani ahi vulanga nchumu ha yena." Isiah 53:3 (ASV) **Hope Translator: Cheryl**

Ngobeni (Giyani, South Africa)

34. From Thoughts of Suicide to Healing

English (Spanish)

"Look at those cheeks, so chubby!" I cannot remember how many times I heard that when I was a little girl. It never felt like a compliment. I was not overweight. I was a healthy girl. But, somehow, I started feeling fat. So I ate less and less.

And then I was diagnosed with anemia, so they gave me medicine that made me hungry. Instead of going for the healthy choices, I ate junk food. And by the end of the summer between sixth and seventh grade, I was overweight.

Way too big to be accepted by my "friends" who had known me since I was six years old. Suddenly, I was by myself. No friends. People who had come to my house for sleepovers laughed at me. I felt like the loneliest person in the planet. My parents didn't notice that something was wrong: their girl had perfect grades in school. But their girl was also watching TV for six to eight hours every day and eating all day long. It became a vicious cycle: my friends laughed at me, I felt lonely, I ate more, I gained weight...

One day, I decided that my life was not worth living. I was on the roof of my two-story house and thought about killing myself. I thought about it for a long time and while I was walking around the edge, my sister told me: "What are you doing there? You are going to fall!" I realized that I didn't want to fall or die, but also that I was not alone. My sister loved me. I sat and cried with her.

Over the next couple of months, I started high school and met friends who liked me for who I was. We would ride bikes, swim, and go dancing. I started losing weight and gaining confidence. I started reading the Bible and praying. I became friends with the rejected ones, keeping in mind my loneliness in middle school, and promising I would never let anyone feel that lonely. It was through this love from others and to others that I started to heal.

Healing is a never-ending process. Sometimes the wounds seem to be still bleeding, and some days they look like an old scar. But in this process, I know that I am not alone and that God *"heals the broken-hearted and binds up their wounds."* *Psalm 147:3 (NIV)*

Hope Writer: Claudia Lizette Aguilar (Atlanta, Georgia, USA)

Spanish (English)
Dios "sana a los que tienen roto el corazón, y les venda las heridas." *Salmo 147:3 (NIV)* **Hope Translator: Claudia Lizette Aguilar (Atlanta, Georgia, USA)**

35. Strength, Courage, and Wisdom

English (Spanish)
In 2008, I was diagnosed with acute lymphoblastic leukemia at the age of 22, after having graduated from college only four months prior. I believe I lived in a state of denial that I even had the "c" word during most of my treatment, because my attitude about it all couldn't have

been more stellar or positive and I got through all of the treatments like a champ and went into remission immediately. I even distinctly remember hearing God tell me "your faith has made you healed." So imagine my surprise when the cancer came back six months shy of my five year "anniversary"!

In October of 2012, my oncologist wanted me to come in and have a biopsy done because my blood counts had been steadily dropping for the previous three to six months. I was coming in to him for follow-up, routine, check-in visits, and that's when I found out that "it" had returned and that I would have to get a stem cell transplant. I was devastated, as I'm sure anyone else would be, and my body's reactions to all of the chemo and radiation that immediately followed the re-diagnosis didn't help matters either. I truly was on an emotional rollercoaster, having internal battles with what I believed to be true and what was happening before my very eyes.

My older sister ended up being a donor match for me, which was a major blessing; and I received her cells on February 6, 2013. Although my time in the hospital was unpretty, to say the very least, God did spare me some of the hardships that I had seen other patients face. To date, I am in complete remission with no evidence or signs of cancerous cells.

I have been in the church and have been a Christian since an early age; and I would be lying if I said that I didn't have questions about Him allowing me to go through all of this a second time... especially when my doctor said that the initial round of treatments back in 2008 and 2009 should have knocked "it" out. But to me, it's like Albert

Camus said, "I'd rather live my life as if there is a God and die to find out that there isn't, than live my life as if there isn't and die to find out there is."

The scripture that I hold fast to and have found comfort in is Jeremiah 30:17a, *"But I will restore you to health and heal your wounds,' declares the Lord."* *(NIV)*

Hope Writer: Sabrina Shelton (Bedford, Virginia, USA)

Spanish (English)
"Porque yo te devolveré la salud, y te sanaré de tus heridas declara el senor." *Jeremias 30:17* **Hope Translator: Rebecca Holderman (Centralia, Washington, USA)**

36. God Kept Me

English (Swahili)
There's a song called "I Almost Let Go," by Kurt Carr. I heard it this morning and it made me really stop and listen to the words: "God held me close, so I wouldn't let go."

I suffer with a type of depression that is more situational than a doomsday daily-living type depression. I only go into it when I'm in a situation that causes me great mental discomfort and confusion. I go into a mindset where I feel so alone and helpless. I feel bound by the current situation and struggle seeing past its passing in days to come. I'm functional at work and around others, but inside I just want to ball up in my bed, stay under the covers, and cry.

Lying in the bed, on the couch, trying to read a book or watch a movie feels like I'm force-feeding positive distractions. It's hard to even eat during this time. I shut down and feel at times like it's a comfort zone as well because time just passes and I just sleep through it.

Hindsight, there was much productivity lost during that time. I was praying, but it felt so shallow. In my praying I felt as if I wasn't exercising my faith in knowing that God would bring me through, and that in turn made me feel worse. I would pray and go right back to that depression. However, I didn't stop; I kept praying and conversing with God and I tried to remind myself of other times I felt this way and made it through.

I know how to help others get out of that mindset but I allow myself to become so consumed by it that it distorts my thinking towards betterment. I would say I'm managing much better now than in the past but, hearing that song this morning, I know why it gets easier and doesn't last as long: God kept and keeps me so I wouldn't and won't let go! That's his promise!

God has so much in store for me, and I'm learning when I look at situations not to ask "why me?" but instead ask "why not me?" God allows us to go through and endure valley-type situations just as he did Job. Job's ability to maintain his faith in who God was in the midst of what he was going through can be challenging but, in the end, God's promises always come to pass.

One thing that gives me great strength is to pray for others. I go through a list in my mind of people I know and don't know, and I just begin to pray and intercede to a degree where my focus changes from my problems towards God being a major blessing in their lives. We never know what someone else is going through – there are situations far worse than what we are enduring.

God is keeping me. In Jeremiah 29:11 he gave his plans for me, "plans to prosper you and not to harm you, plans to give you hope and a future." It's usually not until I am out of the situation that I look back and see that God kept me so I wouldn't let go: I made it through!

No one said this life would be easy, but I believe we must see for ourselves, be a witness, and share with others our testimony of how He kept us and will keep us every day of our lives. See how great our God is in keeping us. His Grace and Mercy will endure forever.

"For I know the plans I have for you," declares the LORD, "plans to prosper you and not to harm you, plans to give you hope and a future." Jeremiah 29: 11 (NIV)

Hope Writer: NaTisha Peacock (Greensboro, North Carolina, USA)

Swahili (English)
"Kwa kuwa naijua mipango niliyonayo kwenu," asema BWANA, "mipango ya kuwajenga na si kuwaharibu, mipango ya kuwapa matumaini katika siku zenu za mwisho." Yeremia 29: 11 (NIV) **Hope Translator: Merchades Method Rutechura (Dar es Salaam, Tanzania, East Africa)**

37. Godly Grief and Sorrows for Growth in Spiritual Life

English (German)
Here in Germany I lay down in bed talking to God, still in

agony from another hard blow in my personal life. I never, ever wanted to believe the secret doings of my husband were real.

In 1998 we took the seventeen-year old girl into our home to work for the Lord. I trained her to sing for the Lord in the Praising and Worship Ministry. That was what my husband wanted. We even treated her like our own daughter in every way.

In short, three years later, that young lady wanted me out of my husband's life, out of my own home, the church and the whole ministry. I didn't sense this coming at all. I wasn't even a bit suspicious.

In our marriage right from the very start, I entrusted everything to my husband, never asking for any single penny for myself. I had married for love and to have a family of my own and not for money or any material things in this world. Little did I know, I was only used for his own ends for eighteen long years! All our monetary assets were withdrawn and deposited in another bank, my name and three of our children's names deleted as beneficiaries. I had no money, not even for medication for the children. Such a hard, painful, cruel, killing, shocking blow!

The unforeseen, severe emotional distress caused me to lose six kilos (thirteen pounds) overnight. I never thought I could lose my most-beloved partner in, since I loved him more than anyone and anything else in this world. But when God himself brought it all into the open years later, there was no way I could not believe him. Deeply hurting in helplessness, total loss and complete poverty, I waited for God's unknown, unusual, extraordinary, supernatural blessings in disguise!

I had been naïve, simply believing every person was really very good. I was totally gullible.

God revealed his goal in my life while I spoke to him in prayer: "not wanting to be loved anymore, but wanting to love, understand, forget and deny myself." It freed me from hurt and bitterness against my ex-husband!

God's reply came while I was silently and patiently waiting, he said, "I have filled you with my strength." What a God we have in Jesus! What a love we have in him! Glory to God in the highest for the blessings in disguise, just because he loves us. That's his very purpose in each of our lives: He allows things to happen to his faithful, obedient servants to change us all into someone he wants us to be, so that he can use us for special occasions in his own ministry while on earth.

"Blessed are those who mourn. They will be comforted."
Matthew 5:4 (GW)

Hope Writer: Adelita V. Maxilom Skrzypek (Kiel, Germany)

German (English)
"Selig die Trauernden; denn sie werden getröstet werden."
Matthew 5,4 (GW) **Hope Translator: Ha Feh (Kiel, Germany)**

38. Hope in the Resurrection!

English (French)
A year ago, around this time, I was leaving a hospital after having visited one of my seminary professors who had been critically ill for months. I had been going to visit, many times without him even knowing that I was there. I would just go, allow myself to be present and pray for God to heal him so that he could live and get back to teaching and transforming students' lives in the classroom.

On this particular night, I stood in the room, reading all of the cards posted around the room which displayed hopeful words of encouragement and get well wishes. In my mind, I began to struggle between the "if" and "when" God's healing would manifest in his life and raise him from his unresponsive state of being. I started saying to myself, "Without faith, it's impossible to please God." So, I determined in that moment that as one who was standing in the gap as an intercessor, I would stop saying, "God, if you would heal…" and start to claim, "God, when you heal…"

I prayed, released a few tears of thanksgiving and expectancy and began to walk to my car. It was a quiet night and there were not too many people out. Still in a posture of reflection and prayer, I heard a voice say to me very clearly, "Faith doesn't trump fate."

Puzzled by the response, I began to question the role of faith in this particular situation and started to give rebuttal. I went on in the spirit of faith believing that God was going to heal my professor and believed nothing different.

A few days later, another professor saw me walking on campus and asked me had I heard. I looked at her puzzled and she stroked my hand telling me that the other professor had just passed a little while earlier that day. She sat with me as I processed the initial shock of hearing the news. After she left and my environment grew quiet, I heard again, "Faith doesn't trump fate." The Spirit began to explain to me that God's will reigns. Faith and hope are intricate parts of our journeys, but the will of God shall not be deterred by our wants and desires. Further, the Spirit said, "you prayed for healing but healing didn't manifest in the form that you desired. You were praying for a physical healing but his healing came in the form of transition and resurrection!"

So, now, I am reminded that Dr. Smith's healing was in the hope of salvation through the love of God in Jesus. The healing was in the transition from flesh to unclothed spirit, from mortality to immortality. The healing was in the hope that those who die a physical death are resurrected to live with God for an eternity.

Coming off of Easter, I realize that the healing is not in the death but in the resurrection! Thus it is essential to have hope. Death is gloomy, dismal, and sad, but our hope must be in the resurrection, in the re-awakening of the spirit after God calls one to draw their last breath on this side of existence. It is the resurrection that manifests the transmission of miraculous, healing, spirit-freeing power.

"You'll be — and experience — a blessing. They won't be able to return the favor, but the favor will be returned — oh, how it will be returned! — at the resurrection of God's people." Luke 14:14 (MSG)

Hope Writer: Ericka S. Dunbar (Atlanta, Georgia, USA)

French (English)

"Vous serez et expérience-une bénédiction. Ils ne seront pas en mesure de retourner la faveur, mais la faveur sera retourné-oh, comment il sera retourné à la résurrection du peuple de Dieu." *Luc 14:14 (MSG)* **Hope Translator: Erika Lobe (Baltimore, Maryland, USA)**

39. They Diagnosed Me with Death, But God Has Called Me to Speak Life

English (Spanish)

Many of you have no idea of what I am going through at the moment; however, I felt compelled to share a portion of what will be my testimony.

Recently, I have been given only a specific amount of time to live, due to being diagnosed with a disorder. Not only that, the doctor even stated to me, "Dameian, this might be a "Come to Jesus Moment" for you. When many people are facing death, all of a sudden they want to run to Jesus." All I could do is smile. He has no idea who I represent in the Kingdom. Even in my situation, God still has the final say-so. So I encourage you to know that even in your situation, God still has the final say-so.

My only reason for wanting to share this is to give someone else hope to endure to the end. Please keep that specific doctor and other leaders in the medical field in prayer over his/her beliefs. For the Bible states, *"For where two or three are gathered together in my name, there am I in the midst of them." Matthew 18:20 (KJV)*

If God will do this for me, He shall do it for you. He has shown me too much to allow me to die during the time frame that has been spoken over my life. Just because God has shown me a vision of my ministry all over the world, this is an indication that I shall not die until that vision comes to pass. I am truly grateful to even have breath in my body to type this at this moment. I pray that this message shall change lives all over the world... even now!

If you died today, would you go to Heaven or to Hell? If you don't know if Heaven is your home, please repeat this small prayer after me: Lord Jesus, I believe that you died on the cross for me; I believe that you rose from the dead; I believe that you are the Only Begotten Son. I want you to come into my life. I want you to change the way I think; I want you to change the way that I live. I want to live for you, God. Today, I make you my King. I surrender my life to you; I surrender my heart to you. Now I am saved. In Jesus name, Amen!

What do you need to do now? Three important first things:

1. Read the Bible.

2. Pray as much as possible every day.

3. Try to find a church that believes in the whole Bible, believes in the practice of the whole New Testament, and believes in the Biblical baptism of the Holy Spirit in a balanced view. Go to church regularly. Be led by the Spirit to find this. Surround yourself with people who are grounded and planted in the Word of God. Whenever you are facing troubled times, these shall be the people who can keep you in covenant prayer. I am so excited that you

decided to make the best investment in your life.

Romans 10:9 reads, *"That if you confess with your mouth the Lord Jesus and believe in your heart that God has raised Him from the dead, you will be saved." (NKJV)*

Blessings! Remember, you may be the only Bible that someone may ever read!

Hope Writer: Pastor Dameian Battle, MBA (Rocky Mount, North Carolina, USA)

Spanish (English)
"Que si confiesas con tu boca al Señor Jesús , y creyeres en tu corazón que Dios le levantó de los muertos, serás salvo ." Romanos 10:09 (NKJV) **Hope Translator: Rebecca Holdermann (Centralia, Washington, USA)**

40. Speaking to Live

English (German)
I was embarrassed to write this: how many African-American women do you know who speak openly about having an eating disorder? We are a culture that encourages curves on a woman – and here I am telling the world that I did all I could to prevent a curvaceous body. Here I am spilling my secret to you – to let you know that you aren't alone and that there really is hope. The moment I surrendered, God freed me. Silence will kill you. It will suffocate you.

I choose to speak in order to live. We all have that "thing" that holds us captive — that secret sin that we think we hide well, the thing that we want to be freed from but are too afraid to live without. My "thing" is food. Yes, you read it correctly, food. I love to eat, but gaining weight is the part I have struggled with. For me, food and fat went hand in hand.

Growing up, I was always the skinny one of the bunch. I held that title until I hit a growth spurt and everything (I mean, EVERYTHING) got bigger. This was not okay with me. I could hide it, right? No one would notice. Wrong! People noticed and were quick to let me know that my adolescent self was gaining weight. I was getting bigger – they made sure I knew it.

I was too naïve to understand that the body goes through changes. I did what would become a downward spiral: I tried to fix it. I wanted to fix whatever was wrong in my body. Fixing it sent me into a fight with bulimia that almost killed me. What do you do when you lose control over what you work so hard to control? The enemy was having a field day with me. My mind felt dark and depressed. No hope flooded my heart – no joy at all.

Psalm 120:1 says, *"In my distress I cried unto the Lord, and he heard me."* (KJV) That scripture will forever hold true for me. I met God on my bathroom floor – and he would change my entire life. One day during a typical binge and purge cycle I began to vomit small specs of blood. It scared me. I cried out to God and prayed that I wouldn't die like this. I had many times told God, "after this time, Lord, I'll never do it again", but this moment was different. I was frightened like never before, shaken at the sight of my own blood. My being in control was killing me, and if I didn't want to die then I had to let Him control this situation. And He did. He heard my cry and He came.

My battle with this disorder is long, hard, and ugly – but I'm so grateful that God didn't let me stay in my filth. I've had my share of times when I fell back into it, but God loosens my grip to hold on while He takes over. He has set me free. By His power, I can live. There are times when I'm unsure and tempted, but I know where to run to. His Word rests in my heart, and that's a place where the lies of Satan, the world and my own flesh cannot dwell.

I want to reassure you that, no matter what you're struggling with, there is healing, there is power, in the name of Jesus. There is freedom, and there is hope. I cried out and He heard me. I now speak because He allowed me to live.

Hope Writer: Ebony D. Holt (Burlington, NC, USA)

German (English)
"Ich rufe zu dem HERRN in meiner Not, und er erhört mich."
Psalm 120, 1 **Hope Translator: Ha Feh (Kiel, Germany)**

Prayer

41. Spirit Song

English (French)
"The Lord is my strength and song, And he has become my salvation." Psalm 118:14 (NKJV)

Throughout our lives we face various challenges. Whether big or small, the fear we are facing in the moment is the challenge we must overcome, and the one that Jesus speaks to–or sings to. I found this out when my spirit began to sing to me one early morning in China.

When I moved to Beijing to live with my college friend, teach English, and experience China, I was both excited and a little lost. I was in my twenties and the world was wide open to me. Partly it was wide open because my fiancée had recently broken up with me.

The plans I had begun forming that stretched into my forever had suddenly disappeared like a wisp of smoke. So I was open to what the world had, and more to the point, what God had for me as I explored the world.

I was told getting a teaching job was easy in China. "Everyone is looking for native English speakers." And, sure enough, within a week I had the promise of a job teaching English about thirty hours a week to first and third graders.

The night before my first day I was nervous. I had never really taught before, officially, and I didn't speak any Chinese. That night I didn't sleep very well, and I kept shooting up prayers for peace and guidance. I remember feeling as though my chest was constricted from the anxiety I held, and I could hardly breathe well.

Compounding the anxiety were the whispered doubts, "What are you doing here, Andrew, in China? Aren't you running away from God? Will God help you be a teacher, when you might be out of his will?"

It was early light, about five a.m., when I awoke through my fitful sleep to a song, clear as day, that was threading itself through the fear in my chest. My own spirit was singing to me, not from my head or my mouth, but from deep within:

"He leadeth me, he leadeth me. By His own hand, he leadeth me." O blessed assurance. Thank you, Jesus.

Hope Writer: Andrew Spidahl (Holland, Michigan, USA)

French (English)
"Le Seigneur est ma force et mon chant. Et il est devenu mon salut." *Psaume 118 :14 (NKJV)* **Hope Translator: Andrew Spidahl (Holland, Michigan, USA)**

42. The Power of Meditation

English (Swahili)
You wake up and turn on the tv or the computer or the radio, and the world comes rushing in on you, and unfortunately, it is usually a rush of negatives. I wonder why more people don't try starting their day with something more positive.

If everyone on the planet started the day with prayer or meditation, I am thinking the entire focus and energy of our planet would instantly "glow with love", sort of like a huge sprinkling of glitter. Once I discovered the life-saving power of meditation, I truly found myself!

It is in meditation that I bask in the glow of my true essence, my spirit, my God-force. It is in that deeply sacred and safe place where I find my connection with the love of God, and that love takes me out into the world. I am more able to see the beauty in the sun as it rises or the flowers as they're blooming, or the smiles of the people on the street.

Do try this at home: Before you even get out of bed every morning, stop and say "thank you for this day," focus on all that you have, intend that your day will unfold with only goodness surrounding you, look for the good in yourself and others and, at the end of the day, before you sleep, focus on all the good you experienced. Say "thank you" again and slip into that place of restful sleep, knowing that the power of love surrounds you… everywhere… all the time!

"Sing to GOD a thanksgiving hymn, play music on your instruments to God." Psalm 147:7 (MSG)

Hope Writer: Debbie Wallace Whittington-Robinson (Mebane, North Carolina, USA)

Swahili (English)
"Mwimbieni Bwana kwa kushukuru, mwimbieni Mungu wetu kwa vinubi." Zaburi 147: 7 (MSG) **Hope Translator: Merchades Method Rutechura (Dar es Salaam, Tanzania, East Africa)**

43. Have You Asked God Yet?

English (Spanish)

I remember it like it was yesterday. We were testing an equipment package for a client in the oil/gas industry. Considering the fact that our company serviced many of the well-known companies, we'd done this before, but not with this specific equipment layout. The client had distinct needs, so the lead engineer tailored a system just for the task at hand.

The first day, all of the technicians assembled to test the system before shipping it to the client. With drawings in tow, we brainstormed, working together to make the system work according to the way the engineer had designed it, but we kept running into issues. Sure, we had the drawings, but it's like something was missing. So, needless to say, we didn't make much progress that day.

On day two, with fresh sets of eyes, we tackled the project again, only to run into a different set of issues. This time, it was the interpretation of the drawings that baffled us. Let's be clear. At the time, I was no novice, boasting 11 years of electronics troubleshooting, not to mention the experienced technicians at my side. But it's like something was hidden. And we just couldn't put our fingers on it. So that day, we went home with nothing accomplished.

The third day, we arrived and the daily meeting convened. As we went around the table taking suggestions, one of the more inexperienced technicians calmly stated, "Let's consult with the engineer who designed the system." And just that quickly, the "aha" moment hit us, as well as the humility that comes with embracing the fact that we truly needed help. We should have considered this much earlier in our troubleshooting process, but so often, we get caught up in our experience and accolade that we subconsciously become puffed up and deny the fact that in all things, we need help.

In life, we can get so used to doing things on our own, trying to "troubleshoot" the issues that we face rather than kneeling in prayer and communicating with the one true and living God that engineered not only you, but the entire Universe, and most importantly, your destiny. Sure we have the Word of God, but without the voice of God, it won't come full circle in our lives.

In this moment, God taught me that no matter what issue I face, even if it seems like I should be able to handle it, seek Him first.

"Trust in the Lord with all your heart, and lean not on your own understanding; In all your ways acknowledge Him, and He shall direct your paths." Proverbs 3: 5-6 (NKJV)

Hope Writer: Zamansky L. Moore (Houston, Texas, USA)

German (English)
"Mit ganzem Herzen vertrau auf den Herrn; bau nicht auf eigene Klugheit; such ihn zu erkennen auf all deinen Wegen, dann ebnet er selbst deine Wege." Sprüche 3,5-6 (NKJV) **Hope Translator: Ha Feh (Kiel, Germany)**

44. Hope Artist Reflection: Snow Journey; Sand Prayers

English (Sepedi)
Hope Artist: Rod Spidahl
Location: Fergus Falls, Minnesota, USA

I travel seul; we journey, wearied
Of Me, myself & I—not three
Ego hungers for His Presence
Butterfly in Pollened Lee . . .

We are sand, just drifting, sifted
We are flakes the wind will shake
Detached, these dry bones lying frozen
Pieced in ice above the lake

Songs without harmonic motion?
Barques on adolescent's sea?
Joi de Vivre found in Being
Woe in we if all are me's

We are snows sifting, drifting
Simple grains the waters rake
Death like lone bones yearning, lying,
Locked immobile 'neath life's lake

Traitorous, betrayed and traitor
Welcomed wounding, healing space
God's attacking hoarded me-somes
Slain and raised in arms of Grace!

Child—I burrowed snows soft comfort
Youth—my toes the beach embraced
Grown, we travel, far, together
Love creates all kindred space.

Snowstorm beckons into calmness,
Cutting sand-smooth agates make!
Let my journey be Communion
Melt my ice and drink the lake!

What is the name of this piece of artwork?
"Snow Journey; Sand Prayers"

What inspired you to create this piece of art?
Being deeply touched by the created earth, the elements of nature and life out-of-doors, I am pulled into and through them as visible words. The help to express how God uses failures and death in me; in us and our ego-driven attempts at community and life to weather us, to inspire and beckon us to be patient, to let the pain have its full effect. Ultimately, these things cannot destroy us, but can shape, mold and reform us; to transform us so we are not afraid to embrace all of life, its beauty and ugliness.

How do you see hope within your artwork?
Mysteriously, there are gospel-impregnated clues scattered in all places. In each seemingly all-frozen pain and isolated death, a grace-melting and a mercy-spring-thaw awaits someone, somehow.

What is one Christian scripture that is connected to your art?
"We know that the whole creation has been groaning as in the pains of childbirth right up to the present time. Not only so, but we ourselves, who have the firstfruits of the Spirit, groan inwardly as we wait eagerly for our adoption as sons, the redemption of our bodies." Romans 8:22-23 (NIV)

How do religion and culture influence your work?
Though this may sound strange to some, religion and culture alternately promise me I can be good enough or shame me that I don't measure up. As I am broken against these and my own expectations, God comes in various Gospel ways and offers hope that transcends culturalisms and false religion. At the same time, I find wonderful love and fascination in experiencing people in cultural expressions other than my own.

Sepedi (English)
"Re a tseba gore hlolego ka moka ga yona e be e tsetla bjalo ka mosadi a e kwa leshoko la pelego go fihla nakong ya bjale. Eupsa ga se hlolego fela e tsetlago; le rena beng re lego dithakangwaga tja Moya o mokgethwa, re llela teng, re ntje re letetje Modimo gore a tle." Baroma 8:22-23 (NIV) **Hope Translator: Warrel Stephen Mothoa (Soweto, South Africa)**

45. Peace of Mind

English (Spanish)
At this very moment I find myself at a state of complete peace. I don't let things bother me to the point where I worry. I may talk about something to get it off my chest, which psychology tells us to do because it causes stress to hold things in that bother you. I even went out and brought the peace sign in every piece of jewelry that I could find. I did this so that I could have some form of peace with me everywhere that I go. The bible says: *"Peace I leave with you; My peace I give to you; not as the world gives, do I give to you. Let not your heart be troubled, nor let it be fearful."* John 14: 27 (NASB77)

Like the song says, "This joy that I have the world didn't give it to me, and the world can't take it away!" I urge you on today to find that peace in whatever circumstance that you're going through! You don't have to play a certain role in life for example: working mom/father, artist, or student. This applies to any and every one.

I especially want to speak to mothers. Mothers, put yourself first, because if you're not healthy then you can't take care of your children and family. They need you to be at your most peaceful state of mind. Not worrying will give you the peace of mind that you're seeking.

Another scripture used to encourage peace says: *"Be anxious for nothing, but in everything by prayer and supplication with thanksgiving let your requests be made known to God. And the peace of God, which surpasses all comprehension, shall guard your hearts and your minds in Christ Jesus." Philippians 4:6-7 (NASB77)*

Hope Writer: Kerri Rigsbee (Kannapolis, North Carolina, USA)

Spanish (English)
"Por nada estéis afanosos; antes bien, en todo, mediante oración y súplica con acción de gracias, sean dadas a conocer vuestras peticiones delante de Dios. Y la paz de Dios, que sobrepasa todo entendimiento, guardará vuestros corazones y vuestras mentes en Cristo Jesús." Filipenses 4:6-7 **Hope Translator: Rebecca Holderman (Centralia, Washington, USA)**

46. We Give You All The Glory

English (Spanish)
Grant us your wisdom oh god of many names and of many faces.

Oh god, you who are truly a divine mystery, beyond our limited capabilities, we invoke the wisdom of those who come before us, we invoke the spirit and mindfulness of Jesus, a spirit of courage and meekness.

Great and wonderful god, grant us your wisdom.

Grant us your wisdom, god of all languages, god of all beings, god of small things, and god of big fat generosity, god of endless love and mercy, show us with your eyes, oh god, the cracks and patches that we have made to get by but that no longer can withstand the bacteria that has grown underneath. Illuminate our spirit oh god, like that of Jesus, help us to see a third way, a way where all parties can win and have dignity, oh god.

Grant us your wisdom, let us draw from our own pains and wounds, let not our eyes become overcast with wool, lest we throw stones at each other, but instead we will draw wisdom from your eyes and your spirit, such that we can recognize the suffering, pain, and causes of angst deep in our core, that we may be able to see that when one part of the body suffers, the whole body suffers! There is no mistake in our interconnectedness — keep us mindful of our whole bodies that make up this testimonies-of-hope community.

God, grant us your wisdom, oh gracious and loving god, that we do not draw lines between ourselves but instead align our minds, passion, and faith with your love and compassion that uplifts — even broken vessels.

Grant us your wisdom oh mothering god and creator; we put ourselves in your hands, your mercy, your grace, and with a listening ear attune to your voice as it comes through those gathered here. With you, we work towards creating and co-creating your vision preordained for us in this time and in this place.

Grant us your wisdom, god. Grant us your wisdom, oh god.

God with this in our hearts, we give you all the glory–

Praise be to God.

"So, whether you eat or drink, or whatever you do, do everything for the glory of God." 1 Corinthians 10:31 (NRSV)

Hope Writer: Reverend Sonsiris Tamayo De-Witt (Hayward, California, USA)

Spanish (English)
"Entonces, ya sea que comáis, que bebáis, o que hagáis cualquiera otra cosa, hacedlo todo para la gloria de Dios." 1 Corintios 10:31 **Hope Translator: Rebecca Holderman (Centralia, Washington, USA)**

47. The Sun Has No Time For Your Broken Heart

English (Xhosa)
Wake up young girl, the sun has no time for your broken heart
Why invite melancholy to share your bed when the beauty of the day awaits you?
You have your heart back in your own hands, don't destroy it with sweaty palms and dripping tears
Those holes it has, only love can fill them.
Open your hand young girl and allow God to work

Wake up young girl, the moon has no time for your broken heart
Why allow the fleeting feeling of pain make your plans for tonight?
The world may have torn off a piece of who you thought you were, but it can never take all of you
You are of God
Let him heal your wounds

Wake up young girl, your child has no time for your broken heart
Why let her weeping be in unison with yours?
She has an entire life of laughter to start with you
The Lord has the power to stop her tears with the sound of your breathing
You hold so much in you young girl, why let a broken heart take that away from you?

Wake up young girl, the Lord is waiting to use you to change the world.

"Peace I leave with you; my peace I give to you. Not as the world gives do I give to you. Let not your hearts be troubled, neither let them be afraid." John 14: 27 (ESV)

Hope Writer: Nwabisa Tolom (Johanessburg, South Africa)

Xhosa (English)
"Ndishiya uxolo kuni; ndininika uxolo lwam; andininiki njengokunika kwehlabathi. Mayingakhathazeki intliziyo yenu, mayingabi nabugwala." John 14:27 **Hope Translator: Sivu Tywabi (Johannesburg, South Africa)**

Relationships

48. The Good Thing, or The God Thing?

English (Malayalam)
I don't crush often, but when I do, I crush pretty hard. Like, thinking of this special someone 24/7 hard. I feel that everyone has had a strong desire for something to be theirs and has thought constantly about that particular thing.

To keep things anonymous, let's just say that I once had a crush on a guy at some point in my life. During our first conversation, he was very attentive, and began discussing his love for Christ unabashedly, something that I found to be uncommon outside of church for guys my age. What is more, he had a great sense of humor, and there was stargazing involved. Needless to say, with the aid of the romantic scenery, I instantly formed a crush. Since I had been talking to God about what a Christ-centered relationship looked like, I took this to mean that He was finally showing me my Boaz.

As usual with my crushes, I daydreamed often and in great detail about how the relationship between the guy and me would begin, what our first (and second, and third) date would be like, and so on. Because I was spending all of my time envisioning a relationship with a Christian guy, I told myself that it was acceptable.

I had been thinking about my crush for a week before we saw each other again. It would be nice to be able to say that we started right where we left off, and that I could see the stars that we gazed upon on that fateful night in his eyes as they sparkled with his excitement to be in my presence. However, that would be false. In short, nothing came of this crush other than a few much-needed lessons.

First off, I learned that, just because a good opportunity comes along in the same area of your life that you've been praying on, it doesn't necessarily mean that it's meant to be. As my pastor once put it, don't mistake the good thing for the God thing. We are often so eager to receive a blessing that we jump to the conclusion that something is meant to be before taking the time to think about if it really is. I could have saved time and energy had I allowed myself to think less about where the first date would be held and more about whether or not this guy was for me, and if I was even ready for a relationship.

Related to this lesson is the idea of understanding God's timing. I let my desire to find a Christian guy cause me to try and make it happen prematurely. As previously stated, this was quite the fruitless endeavor. I also allowed my crush to keep me from doing more productive things, like working on my personal walk with Christ and discovering who I am meant to be in Him. Funny thing is, working on bettering myself and growing in my relationship with God helps to prepare me for a relationship with a guy. I got so distracted by what I wanted that I was hindering myself from attaining that very thing.

In no way am I saying that it is wrong to have a crush, or to want something. However, it becomes problematic when this wanting hinders you from seeing God's plan and from doing what He wants you to do. When you allow God to control your life rather than your desires, then He will indeed give you the (good) desires of your heart, and then some.

"Take delight in the LORD, and he will give you your heart's desires." Psalm 37:4 (NLT)

Hope Writer: Niya Tanyi (Los Angeles, California, USA)

Malayalam (English)
"Yehovayil thanne rasichu kolka; avan ninte hridhayathile agrahangale ninakku tharum." Sangeerthanangal 37:4 (NLT)
Hope Translator: Gladson Thomas (Kottayam, Kerala, India)

49. Beware of Deception

English (Haitian Creole)
I'm sure we are all familiar with the quote, "not everything that glitters is gold," and the same principle holds true in many different ways. Every coin has two sides, every story has two versions, everything that looks real is not real and not every sign or word is from God.

If we do not learn to discern between good and evil and between right and wrong and to tell truth from lies and God's ways from our ways, we will be in trouble.

We are living in a fallen world with a lot of deception around us, and this is no time to be gullible. The Bible teaches us to try every spirit and this is something that should be a part of our nature by default. Not every spirit is of God and not everyone that says 'God' means God. So, too, the reality remains that not every opportunity is from God, and everything that seems right in our own eyes is not always right.

The Bible tells us that there is a way that seems right to a man but at the end is destruction. The devil has the power to appear in any form he chooses, even as an 'angel of light' – so I can't stress this enough: discern, discern, discern, and beware of deception. That is the devil's ultimate goal: to deceive, distract and detour or to kill, steal and destroy.

My encouragement to you is in all your ways, acknowledge him and allow him to direct your path. Do not judge a thing by the way it appears to be, pray for the spirit of discernment, and learn to see things through the eyes of the spirit. Do not judge a book by its cover but rather by the contents written within. Sensual wisdom and spiritual wisdom both have their place, but seek the latter. Forget about what you think and embrace God's standards.

"In all thy ways acknowledge him, and he shall direct thy paths."
Proverbs 3:6 (KJV)

Hope Writer: Author Terry-Ann Scott (Mandeville, Jamaica, West Indies)

Haitian Creole (English)
"Nan tou sa w'ap fè rekonèt li, li pral dirije chemen ou." Pwoveb *3:6 (KJV)* **Hope Translator: Kirk Louis (Midwest City, Oklahoma, USA)**

50. "I Am A Wise Woman"

English (German)
I am a wise woman! I have learned countless lessons that burned and hurt, but got my attention. The other day my

little grandson asked me what an idiot was. I giggled and told him my truth: an idiot is someone who never chooses to learn from their mistakes. I also told him we all make mistakes, but it's so important to learn from them.

Every mistake I have made, I hope I learned to not repeat it! That is why I can profess to be a wise woman. I have learned, and what we truly learn, we never forget. As I tell my grown children, as well as my grandson, "you have two choices every single day: you can choose to live in the positive or you can live in the negative... either way, it is your choice!"

For me, learning this lesson was a turning point in my life. I could no longer look for scapegoats. My choice as to how I would live was my choice. I had to learn to take ownership for myself. The result? I always choose the positive and THAT makes me the wise and happy woman that I am!

"Blessed is the one who finds wisdom and the one who obtains understanding." Proverbs 3: 13 (GW)

Hope Writer: Debbie Wallace Whittington-Robinson (Mebane, North Carolina, USA)

German (English)
"Glückselig der Mensch, der Weisheit gefunden hat, und der Mensch, der Verständnis erlangt." Sprüche: 3, 13 (GW) **Hope Translator: Ha Feh (Kiel, Germany)**

51. Humanity

English (Spanish)
"You cannot shake hands with a clenched fist." ~ Indira Gandhi

The quote above, this proverbs of sorts, evoked the following poem.

Where is the humanity?
Is it in our clenched fist?
Does it lay between ethnic and religious tensions?

We cannot shake hands with clenched fists
The fighting, killing, dying, loss, grief
Brings us anger and denial
Can it bring rebirth?
Can it transform hate and reconcile?

Can it bring an unclenched fist?

Rage, injustice, plunged streets are
filled and flooded with the consequences
of our choices—
our unbelief!

Order!
Chaos!
Is it one and same when there is politics, hierarchy, religiosity, and dominance?

Can we shake hands with a clenched fist?

What do we do?

We are the faithful
women and men of God,
servants of the lord,
with authority over priestly duties,
and blessed sacraments

Questions arise—
Where is our authenticity?
Our integrity?
Our faith and life energy?
Do we question the hands that make fist?
That threaten while promising order?
Is it a promise or a myth?
Do we question it only when it does not mess
with our ease to roam and walk our own streets –
to play and love under the guise of peace

But a clenched fist cannot shake hands

Or – is it that we don't understand our own humanity?

All along I looked for it
I seeked and I seeked –
I found it — inside, me
now, I can see it
in you
and you in me –

So, where is our humanity?
– Can we see it in our enemy?

"God makes his people strong. God gives his people peace."
Psalm 29:11 (MSG)

Hope Writer: Rev. Sonsiris Tamayo-DeWitt (Hayward, California, USA)

Spanish (English)
"El Senor dará fuerza a su pueblo. El Senor bendecirá a su pueblo con paz." *Salmos 29:11 (MSG)* **Hope Translator: Rebecca Holderman (Centralia, Washington, USA)**

52. Hope Artist Reflection: Genesis

English (Jamaican Patois)
Hope Artist: Junior Versailles
Location: Sandy Point, Saint Kitts, West Indies

What is the name of this piece of artwork?
"Genesis"

What inspired you to create this piece of art?
The beginning, Genesis, in the Christian Bible. Everything has a beginning story.

How do you see hope within your artwork?
I see hope within my artwork like food is to one's body. Good art makes you smile and inspires anyone that sees or hears it. It makes us better people!

What is one Christian scripture that is connected to your art?
This scripture is one of the most cleansing scriptures my God ever gave to me. *"Blessed is the man who does not walk in the counsel of the wicked or stand in the way of sinners or sit in the seat of mockers." Psalm 1:1 (NIV)*

How do religion and culture influence your work?
My art is my culture. If you want to call it religion we could talk about that!

Jamaican Patois (English)
"Enie bady who nuh fallaw wicked people advise, an nuh keep cumpiny wid sinna man or ungadly people, an nuh siddung wid people weh luv fi run off dem mowt and chat foolishniss, dem people deh reely blessed!" Psalm 1:1 (NIV) **Hope Translator: Dr. Stephanie Fletcher (Sydney, New South Wales, Australia)**

53. Breaking Bread

English (French)
It was Sunday. In Germany, places shut down on Sundays. Our bicycle touring group was winding its way southward, and we were in need of a drinking water refill.

It was Sunday. It was also two weeks since we'd left Michigan. By this time I was beginning to feel a longing for some spiritual rejuvenation. It's not that our experience so far had been devoid of spiritual encounters. It was more that I felt a strange longing to be among fellow worshipers. I kind of wanted to be in church. I wanted to read sacred texts, to pause in prayer, to sing, to let go and just be.

We turned our bikes toward a small town. As we approached, Devin informed us that there was no gas station – our usual stop for a faucet, and our best guess for something open on a Sunday morning in provincial Germany. We were tired, so we decided to continue looking around for some sign of a water pump. Just then, I spotted a man getting on his bicycle outside of his house. I pulled our heavily laden tandem to a stop in front of the driveway, and turned to look at Kallie. (She spoke German.) She asked if he knew of some place where we might be able to fill our water bottles. He responded, "You can fill them here. Come in."

His wife welcomed us at the door. Her English was excellent and her demeanor calm. Their house was beautiful. I filled a few bottles at the kitchen sink while admiring the beauty of the place, as well as the hospitality of this couple. We were on our way out, thanking them, when the husband asked if we wanted any coffee. "It would be nice," I told him, "but we're trying to make it to Freiburg."

"Can you stay for only ten minutes? The press is coming, they want to do a small story." To that I could only respond, "Yes, okay!" Within minutes we were all sitting around the kitchen table, with coffee, bread, and a reporter asking questions. This was a water stop we hadn't bargained for!

The couple were generous hosts. I could feel my heart expanding. We even broke out the musical instruments we were carrying to play a small concert. Our first song "Ghost Riders" happened to be Ute's favorite. After taking pictures and negotiating contact info, we bid them farewell and left, strengthened and joyful.

It wasn't until well down the trail that I realized the significance of that Sunday morning hospitality to my own spirit, as a Christian longing for an experience of worship. I realized that we had had a sort of holy communion. We were welcomed to the table, we shared our stories, we ate the bread and drank the coffee, we sang, and we were sent off with a blessing and our bottles full of water.

Didn't Christ say in a parable "I was hungry, and you gave me something to eat; I was thirsty, and you gave me something to drink; I was a stranger, and you welcomed me in?"

And I was left with this strange and wonderful phrase echoing within my soul: "He will be known in the breaking of the bread."

"Then the two went over everything that happened on the road and how they recognized him when he broke the bread." Luke 24:35 (MSG)

Hope Writer: Andrew Spidahl (Holland, Michigan, USA)

French (English)
"Puis les deux sont allés sur tout ce qui s'est passé sur la route et comment ils l'avaient reconnu quand il rompit le pain." Luc 24:35 (MSG) **Hope Translator: Erika Lobe (Baltimore, Maryland, USA)**

54. God Wants Your Heart

English (Filipino)
Ever felt like you can't handle reality anymore? "What's next, kick me again while I'm down, won't you?" About 3 months ago, I'd found myself in the most horrible of conditions.

Everything I'd ever feared would happen, everything that could go wrong, all went wrong at the same time. This was already after a long and difficult year. It was as though I'd lost my luck.

I learnt to differentiate between luck and grace. You can run out of luck. God's grace is new every morning.

One of my fears was failure. I'd been part of the top 5 students all my high school life. I couldn't imagine ever failing. You can guess – it happened. The first year in university, opening that report card, I couldn't believe it. I cried, became depressed, and lost all hope – like I was not a child of the living God.

I was worried about what people would say. I feared I'd lose my friends. I felt betrayed by God, felt like he didn't hear me when I prayed. Felt like my life was over. I lost my sponsor as well. What was going to happen with my school fees?

My problem was that I'd fallen into the trap – living like God owes me a favour. I started comparing myself to others. "But God, I serve You, yet I don't succeed. That one doesn't even go to church and You're blessing him."

God used this to rectify the flaws in my relationship with Him. I realized I'd placed my joy on things of this world; my career had become more important to me than God was. Pleasing people and looking good was my priority, rather than my reputation with my God.

God was seeking intimacy with me; he wanted my heart. And so I surrendered my heart. He put it back together. I poured my soul out to Him through prayer. Made Him the center of my life. If it's not about Jesus, then it's not worth it.

I hurt no more now. He makes a way where it seems there is no way. I'm back at school now, doing very well. His thoughts are not our thoughts. His plans for our lives never fail. It may look like that in the world, but He knows the beginning from the end.

All things work together for our good with God. Why seek acceptance from men and women? The word says God approves of you, faults and all. I know that God loves me with no conditions. Just because things go wrong doesn't mean his love changes. I've learnt that my efforts don't affect how God treats me.

"Because of the Lord's great love we are not consumed, for his compassions never fail." Lamentations 3:22 (NIV)

I've since learnt that failing is not as bad as I'd made it out to be. In fact it's a stepping stone. God can use me to help others in this area. Many successful people in the world have failed before to get where they are. It's a matter of how you deal with it. Let fear overwhelm you – or stand up and continue walking.

My relationship with God gets better every day now. I'm learning to understand Him better. I'm also happier now. I know that my attempt may fail, but I'll never fail to attempt.

I choose not to accept the false boundaries and limitations created by the past. No matter what, God will always be God. He will always sit on the throne. I've learnt to praise him through my circumstances!

Hope Writer: Paseka Khosa (Johannesburg, South Africa)

Filipino (English)
"Sa mga kaawaan nga ng Panginoon ay hindi tayo nalipol, sapagka't ang kaniyang mga habag ay hindi nauubos." Mga Panaghoy 3:22 **Hope Translator: Rose Renie Canlas (Baguio City, Phillipines)**

55. I Once Had a Broken Heart

English (Afrikaans)
Last year I went through a break up that left me feeling

lost. I was together with a great guy for almost three years. I was absolutely certain that this was the man God had chosen for me to one day marry. I always believed he felt the same.

However, our relationship reached a point where he felt like he could no longer be with me. When he told me this I was scared of what life would be like without him. Would I still know who I am? Had everything in my life been less than I'd thought it was? I was hurt. No – I was absolutely shattered.

I remembered that no man had the power to decide what makes me smile or cry. No man had the power to dictate what my life would be. Only God and God alone has that power.

So I prayed. With all my strength and honesty I prayed. I rebuilt my relationship with God. It was not easy letting go of something you thought would be forever, and to this day I'm not entirely sure why that relationship ended.

But I know that God has a plan for my life. And I understand that that man had served his purpose in my life. I learnt to accept that I will never have all the answers, but faith in the Lord and His plan is all I need.

God knows each of our hearts. He also knows that each of our spiritual journeys are completely unique. At that time He put people in my life He could speak through. I had the complete comfort and support of friends and family.

I have a wonderful church that showed me support without any judgment. With all these amazing people around me, I heard God's voice the loudest when He spoke to me through what I love to do the most, which is writing. He inspired words in me that would help me heal.

I believed in love. All forms of love. Even without the love of that specific guy, I never felt any less love in my life. I knew that while my heart may be broken for a moment, the promise God has for my life is greater than any pain I was feeling.

"When the righteous cry for help, the Lord hears and delivers them out of all their troubles. The Lord is near to the brokenhearted and saves the crushed in spirit. Many are the afflictions of the righteous, but the Lord delivers him out of them all. He keeps all his bones; not one of them is broken." Psalm 34: 17-20 (ESV)

Hope Writer: Nwabisa Tolom (Johannesburg, South Africa)

Afrikaans (English)
"Die aangesig van die Here is teen die kwaaddoeners,om hulle gedagtenis van die aarde uit te noeim Hulle roep en die Here hoor, en Hy red hulle uit die wat gebroke is van hart, en Hy verlos die wat verslae is van gees. Menigvuldig is die teespoede van die regverdige, maar uit die almal red die Here hom." Psalm 34 17-20 (Die Ganse Heilige Skrif Bible, 1940) **Hope Translator: Roxanne Van Wyk (Durban, South Africa)**

56. Hope Artist Reflection: Embracing Mother of Hope

English (Filipino)
Hope Artist: Rowena "Apol" Laxamana-Sta. Rosa
Location: Imus Cavite City, Phillipines

What is the name of this piece of artwork?
"Embracing Mother of Hope"

What inspired you to create this piece of artwork?
This piece of art gives inspiration to me through remembering our mother's or "ilaw ng tahanan" light of the home (a Filipino idiom describing the mother). I am a mother too, who has many responsibilities and duties inside and outside the house. As a mother we want the best for our family – most of all the love and care. I always hug my daughter. And seeing children on the streets without their mother, or father, makes me sad.

How do you see hope within your artwork?
The mother embracing her child shows hope through love

and care. When a mother embraces her child it is priceless and timeless. I believe that it is the most powerful source of love when you hug and kiss your child. I see hope when a mother really cares not only about her child, but also her surroundings and nature as well. The painting shares the love of life.

What is one Christian scripture that is connected to your art?

"Then he took a little child and put it among them; and taking it in his arms, he said to them, 'Whoever welcomes one such child in my name welcomes me, and whoever welcomes me welcomes not me but the one who sent me.'" Mark 9: 36 – 37 (NRSV)

How do religion and culture influence your work?

As a Christian and a mother I make reflections through sketching and painting, whenever I imagine and create my piece. So let us embrace our children because it gives us hope and strength to live and to love. We are all God's children who embrace Him.

Filipino (English)

"At kinuha niya ang isang maliit na bata, at inilagay sa gitna nila: at siya'y kaniyang kinalong, na sa kanila'y sinabi niya, Ang sinomang tumanggap sa isa sa mga ganitong maliliit na bata sa aking pangalan, ay ako ang tinatanggap: at ang sinomang tumanggap sa akin, ay hindi ako ang tinatanggap, kundi yaong sa aki'y nagsugo." Marcos 9: 36 –37 **Hope Translator: Rose Renie Canlas (Baguio City, Phillipines)**

57. Daddy's Baby

English (Xhosa)
Not too long ago, I took a work trip out of the country. For those of you that travel internationally, you can relate to the very long flight that you have to endure to reach your final destination. Well, after a month, I was finally boarding my return flight, quite excited to rejoin my loved ones in Houston, as I had missed them dearly.

I was under the impression that I would have an entire row to myself on the plane, because there weren't many people checking in for this flight in particular. Boy, was I wrong! It actually ended up being an almost fully-booked flight.

As we all boarded the craft a Brazilian father and his very young and rambunctious daughter accompanied me, sitting on my row. Instantly, I began to hope and pray that the child would go to sleep. Very selfish of me, I know, but I was really looking forward to spending that 10-hour overnight flight in slumber.

Now, when I was raised, we got a spanking for anything and everything. So I expected at least a strong scolding when the child began to act out. But the father lovingly spoke to her in a calm voice.

I could tell that he may have been a little irritated, but his daughter was treated with the utmost care. I marveled at how patient he was, how loving and delicate he was, ever so careful with her.

When it was time to eat, he fed her, gave her apple juice, and soon after she got sleepy, he patted her to sleep. And I was in awe at how he lightly rubbed her head of golden locks and looked intently at the child until she slept. It was so pure.

God taught me such a valuable lesson on that flight. His love for us transcends our difficult moments. His hand is always on us to lovingly guide us, shaping us in His wise care for us.

He comforts us when we are sleeping. He never sleeps nor slumbers, but he is attentive to us and affectionate to his own children. He protects us during the night. As the child rested in her daddy's arms, my heart began to melt at all these beautiful revelations of a father's love.

I encourage you to let God father you. When you are a little difficult, don't immediately expect God's wrath. God is experienced and knows just how to handle you, regardless of how others feel.

As your life ascends from its runway, God is there to comfort you through your turbulence, quiet your fears and allow you to rest in Him. Trust in Him as your guardian today!

"So you have not received a spirit that makes you fearful slaves. Instead, you received God's Spirit when he adopted you as his own children. Now we call him, 'Abba, Father.'" –Romans 8:15 *(NLT)*

Hope Writer: Zamansky L. Moore (Houston, Texas, USA)

Xhosa (English)
"Kuba anamkelanga moya wabukhoboka, ukuba nibuye noyike; namkele umoyawokwenziwa oonyana, esidanduluka ngawo sithi,

Abha, Bawo." *Romans 8:15 (NLT)* **Hope Translator: Sivu Tywabi (Johanessburg, South Africa)**

Joy

58. Hope Artist Reflection: Opening of Lilac Sniffing Season!

English (French)
Hope Artist: Rod Spidahl
Location: Fergus Falls, Minnesota, USA

Across the town, across the field,
my nose was up; winter's body must yield.
Pedaling for scent, I ignored the storm
Pursuing and driven in Spring-fever form.
With memories crowding ahead of the rain –
somewhere out there were Lilacs to gain!

In parts per million my nostrils twitched at
Dandelion, Plum, Apple, Forsythia and Tulip.
Crab-apples and more of delectable stripe—
Uff-Dah! Not that thawing manure so ripe!
Away-ward and quickly, out in circular style,
I pump hard, I strain for, the spring lilac smile.

Serendipitously now, in alley un-kept
(after judging folks round here as inept
at Lilac appreciation; that inhalable joy)
my glance found leaf-form; then perfumed alloy.
Oh, yes, Lilac, you Lilac, so pur-ple-ly blessed,
of all forms of nose joy, in spring, you're the best!

So slyly and stealthy I slipped off a slip,
tucked it in backpack and then home in a zip!
Shared goodness grows friendship and sweet joys abound.

Compound leaf and flowerets speak community
sounds.

Instructed and humbled and awed do I write
In Creator gifts we blossom—such meekness, such might!

What is the name of this piece of artwork?
"Opening of Lilac Sniffing Season!"

What inspired you to create this piece of art?
The joy of springtime scents and life returning in a
northern climate like Minnesota creates what is truly
called "Spring Fever." This poem is a slice of those days
when my college bicycle comes off the hangers in the
garage and I might go exploring what is blossoming, just
on a whim. Like most writing, this was not planned but
just "given" as I rode on that spring day, thinking of
friends and enjoying Creation's larger community coming
alive, again, after a long winter.

How do you see hope within your artwork?
The unspoken words of scented lilac blossoms "shout" at
me to listen with my whole being. While I may go on a
bike ride or walk to get away or pray or sing out my
burdens into the wind and road, there seem to be
surprisingly refreshing God-incidences that I come home
to tell others about.

**What is one Christian scripture that is connected to your
art?**
*"The heavens are telling of the glory of God; And their expanse
is declaring the work of His hands." –Psalm 19:1 (NASB)*

How do religion and culture influence your work?
Religious themes are transcendent ones, springing from
the common things we live among and then taking those
things as vehicles, as metaphors and as pictures that allow

us to get beyond self and be in touch with what we often don't see, but is always there –God-Life and God's self.

Cultures are built on collective words and actions between a group of people with shared interests on an ongoing basis. These shared experiences become memories we build upon. Cultures and religions are most healthy when they allow themselves to be instructed by the life God has created: pure gifts, like the love of God in Christ. Setting our minds on such things by getting out to observe Creation is healthy and it brings hope and joy!

French (English)
"Les cieux racontent la gloire de Dieu; Et l'étendue manifeste l'œuvre de ses mains." *Psaume 19:01 (NASB)* **Hope Translator: Erika Lobe (Baltimore, Maryland, USA)**

59. As Summer Approaches

English (Spanish)
As summer approaches and outdoor activities beckon, many people, especially women, cringe in anticipation of stepping out of the winter clothes – which cover so well – into lighter, more revealing summer clothes.

As I hear more and more women (and girls) vocalize their fears of this, I am struck by the sadness it brings. Remember playing as a child, in the summer heat and never once worrying about how you looked? It was so much more about having fun. The good news is, it can still be that way!

But we have to stop long enough to take stock of all that

we are, all that we have – especially our health! Shame on us for disliking our precious bodies! They are the best machines we will ever own! They deserve our respect and our love!

Martha Graham, the famous modern dance pioneer, said, "Your body is a sacred garment." Truer words were never spoken!

And above all else, remember that your body serves as the temple for your spirit. Breathe in all that is good, and let God surround you with a very warm and very strong spirit hug of love! Love yourself into magnificence!

"You realize, don't you, that you are the temple of God, and God himself is present in you?" 1 Corinthians 3:16 (MSG)

Hope Writer: Debbie Wallace Whittington-Robinson (Mebane, North Carolina, USA)

Spanish (English)
"¿No sabéis que sois templo de Dios y que el Espíritu de Dios habita en vosotros?" 1 Corintios 3:16 (MSG) **Hope Translator: Rebecca Holderman (Centralia, Washington, USA)**

60. Your Joy Is Your Sorrow Unmasked

English (Haitian Creole)
"Your Joy is Your Sorrow Unmasked." –Kahlil Gibran

Tears stream from my eyes. I cannot stop them; I cannot hide them; I cannot deny them. It is April 2009, 3 months shy of my 2-year Anniversary as a Peace Corps Volunteer.

I am pregnant – an unplanned and life changing revelation.

I board a plane and return home to the United States. And as one can imagine, I am wading through a complex set of decisions and dilemmas, battling with confusion, regret, loss, fear, anger, and pain.

In this time, I find myself in Jeremiah 31:19: "After I strayed, I repented; after I came to understand, I beat my breast. I was ashamed and humiliated because I bore the disgrace of my youth."

And in the Lord's great love and mercy, He held me fast and close. He gave me strength to face what felt like insurmountable after insurmountable steps toward reconciliation. I chose life. Praise God. I chose to walk with hope and prayer. Praise God. And though at this time in my spiritual maturity I was but a babe, I found God. Praise God!

September 24, 2009. She is here. My precious daughter, Malaya, is born. Though I still have many large pieces of my life to completely surrender to God, in those first moments of watching life spring forth before me, I stand in awe of God's great glory. As I look into the eyes of my child, resounding joy jumps out of my soul.

Her fingers. Her toes. Her eyes. Her lips. I am overcome with joy and peace. We are enveloped in the love of the Father. I am humbled. I am encouraged. And I am strengthened for the journey ahead.

Today, Malaya is 3 years, 4 months, and 15 days old. Motherhood has blessed me and tested me – and most importantly, it has brought me into an intimate relationship with my Creator. I have a lifetime of growth ahead of me, and yet I sit comforted and rest assured in the precepts and promises of the Father.

I will not deny: the choices were not easy, nor was the pain light. I am still on a journey of healing and faith.

But, I can affirm, with my whole being, that if you hand your life over to God, He will keep you, He will comfort you, and He will restore you in the great and holy plan He has for your life. He will take you out of the very ashes of your sorrow and walk with you, day by day, into a fullness of joy.

Please, dear ones, those of you suffering with the weight of your sins, come to the Lord. Give it to Him. Repent of your ways and seek Him. And in Him you will find healing and joy and something truly miraculous.

As God proclaims: *"I will turn their mourning into gladness; I will give them comfort and joy instead of sorrow." – Jeremiah 31: 13b (NIV)*

Hope Writer: Jasmine Joy Landry (High Rolls, New Mexico, USA)

Haitian Creole (English)
"M'ap wete lapenn yo nan kè kontan; Mwen pral ba yo konfò ak kè kontan olye pou yo lapenn." Jeremi 31: 13b (NIV) **Hope Translator: Kirk Louis (Midwest City, Oklahoma, USA)**

61. Hope Artist Reflection: Sunset of Paradise

English (French)
Hope Artist: Erika Lobe
Location: Baltimore, Maryland, USA

What is the name of this piece of artwork?
"Sunset of Paradise

What inspired you to create this piece of art?
When it comes to painting, I'm always attracted to bright, vibrant colors. I also really love silhouettes and the contrast of the light and dark. Naturally, a gorgeous sunset is full of beautiful colors – so I started with that idea and it just blossomed into this scene.

How do you see hope within your artwork?
Hope, for me, can be described as seeing the light at the end of the tunnel. When you are going through something, it's comforting to know that it will eventually pass and

there are brighter days ahead.

What is one Christian scripture that is connected to your art?

"No one lights a lamp and puts it in a place where it will be hidden, or under a bowl. Instead he puts it on its stand, so that those who come in may see the light. Your eye is the lamp of your body. When your eyes are good, your whole body also is full of light. But when they are bad, your body also is full of darkness. See to it, then, that the light within you is not darkness." – Luke 11: 33-35 (NIV)

How do religion and culture influence your work?

My surroundings impact my art work: the things that I touch, feel, and see. Religion and culture also inherently show up in my art.

French (English)

"On n'allume pas une lampe pour la met dans un endroit où il sera caché ou sous un bol. Au lieu de cela il la met sur un table, afin que ceux qui entrent voient la lumière. Ton oeil est la lampe de ton corps. quand vos yeux sont bons, tout ton corps est aussi plein de lumière. Mais quand ils sont mauvais, ton corps est dans les ténèbres. Veillez à ce donc que la lumière à l'intérieur de toi ne soit ténèbres." Luc 11: 33-35 (NIV) **Hope Translator: Erika Lobe (Baltimore, Maryland, USA)**

62. Rejoicing in His Creation

English (Haitian Creole)

I sit upon the back step and watch the clothes flutter in the wind, sun glazing my skin, and my daughter exploring the tiniest of creations in the soil with her "bug magnifying glass."

I simply love hanging clothes on the clothesline – a grounding ritual that engages my mind, body, and spirit. There's just something about watching the elements doing their work so effortlessly – the sun shining, the wind blowing, the water evaporating.

There is something very satisfying in being present in this process and being in harmony with it – fulfilling my purpose, my work, within the harmony of this system. This is lovely. This brings me delight.

Yes, to the smallest details of existence, isn't it glorious to watch His handiwork? Yes, to see his purposes in the natural world around us and delight in it.

As it is beautifully penned in *Psalm 147:7-8*, *"Sing unto the Lord with thanksgiving; sing praise upon the harp unto our God: Who covereth the heaven with clouds, who prepareth rain for the earth, who maketh grass to grow upon the mountains."* *(KJV)* Isn't Our Creator a great artist?

As the season turns, I pray you each rejoice in the Lord's work all around us. That you breathe it in deeply. That you feel nourished by it. That you revel in it. That you find Him there, in creation, in your life, today.

Hope Writer: Jasmine Joy Landry (High Rolls, New Mexico, USA)

Haitian Creole (English)
"Chante pou Seyè a ak di Bondye mèsi; chante sou gita a pou Bondye nou an: Se li ki kouvri syèl la ak nwaj, ki moun ki pare lapli pou tè a, ki moun ki fè zèb pouse sou mòn yo." Sòm 147:7-8

(KJV) **Hope Translator: Kirk Louis (Midwest City, Oklahoma, USA)**

63. God I Give You Thanks

English (Spanish)
"Better a little with the fear of the Lord, than great wealth with turmoil." *Proverbs 15:16 (NIV)*

In my vocation as a hospital Chaplain, I witness daily people in the deepest crisis of their lives. In moments of crisis, people can be so busy looking for a spectacular revelation of the miracle-working God that they are not able to see God at work in the common, everyday things.

Yes, in times of crisis, I "go there" too. What else does one do, when brokenness, fear, anxiety and even death stare you in the face? You turn to the miracle-working God and pray for that healing that you think will fix the crisis. Don't get me wrong now... God does answer prayers!

We spend our energy hoping, praying and looking for that BIG miracle. As the old cliché goes, *I been so broke, I couldn't pay attention.* I needed a real payday. Spiritual, emotional and physical deaths have all taken their turns staring me in the face.

I prayed to the God of second and third chances of life . . . I wanted to live! I wished upon a star that I was Bewitched and could wiggle my nose for instant healing or money. But NO . . . God sent me some people. What?

I immediately knew God was either not listening to me or I

had prayed the wrong prayer or something. I had prayed for healing/money... not people. There must have been some mistake. In my mind, the people were mere mortals like me. What could they do? I asked for some big things, but what about the small things?

Only when we take the time to appreciate the small blessings from God, will we truly see how God is already at work in our lives. The wonder of friendship, the kindness of strangers, and an understanding heart are all expressions of the greatness and blessings of God.

These small things were the vehicles of healing for the crisis in my life. Hallelujah . . . God was listening and working it all out just for me. I had poverty of spirit and health, but the kingdom of God was mine. God will give you rest, beauty, and riches. Just ask and watch the trinkets begin to appear.

These and other testimonies of my life have led me to not take anyone or anything for granted. I encourage you today to give God thanks for blessings, that you may unlock the treasure room of God and fill your life with new beauty and riches.

Prayer:

I praise and thank you gracious God, for the small things that make each day so delightful. Help me to not take daily blessings for granted.

Hope Writer: Georgia Chambers (Houston, Texas, USA)

Spanish (English)
"Mejor es lo poco con el temor del Senor, que gran tesoro y

turbación con él." *Proverbios 15:16* **Hope Translator: Rebecca Holderman (Centralia, Washington, USA)**

64. Feels Like The First Time

English (Xhosa)
Recently, Grayson Clamp, a three-year-old boy from North Carolina who was born deaf, became the first child in the United States to receive an auditory brain stem implant. After his surgery, he was captured on video hearing his father's voice for the first time.

His facial expression was priceless. His face lit up as if he'd just opened his very first Christmas gift, the gift he'd always wanted. As he heard his father's voice, he also heard for the first time his father tell him that he loved him. As I watched this little boy react in such an excited way to hearing his father's voice, I became overwhelmed.

I thought about how excited I was the first time I felt the presence of God. It was as if God was telling me that He loved me and I was hearing it for the first time. I grew up in church and with an understanding of the supremacy of God.

But it wasn't until I was much older and had experienced life as an adult that I truly knew what it meant to know God and to hear God's voice. As I learned how to tune in to God, I realized that God was always present with me.

I often experience God's presence in many different places. I see trees swaying in the wind or birds flying in a formation and realize that God is present.

I also remember sitting in the hospital all night waiting to see my niece for the first time and thinking of how loving and present God is, all the time and everywhere. So, it was no surprise to me that when this little boy heard his father's voice for the first time, he was happy, joyful, excited, and surprised.

Those are all the feelings we should experience when we experience God for the first time. What is important, though, is to never lose that feeling. Each time we encounter God, it should feel like the first time. We should not allow life's circumstances and situations to cause us to ever take God's presence for granted.

I'm sure that as little Grayson grows older and becomes accustomed to the ability to hear as a regular part of his life, he will sometimes be reminded of the first time and have a renewed appreciation for his gift of hearing.

Prayer:

Lord God, help us to always be grateful for Your presence in our lives. Help us, God, to see You in every living thing and be filled with excitement by the fact that You are always with us. Help us to never take Your presence for granted. Amen.

"In everything give thanks: for this is the will of God in Christ Jesus to you-ward." 1 Thessalonians 5:18 (ASV)

Hope Writer: Margaret A. Brunson (Raleigh, North Carolina, USA)

Xhosa (English)
"Ezintweni zonke bulelani; kuba oko kukuthanda kukaThixo kuKristu Yesu ngani." Thessalonians 5:18 **Hope Translator: Sivu Tywabi (Johannesburg, South Africa)**

65. Hope Artist Reflection: Maple Syruped

English (French)
Hope Artist: Rod Spidahl
Location: Fergus Falls, Minnesota, USA

Warmed and
maple syruped glances
smite the waffle-souled fellow,
leaving him bettered,
golden-browned buttery
and totally pancake-smitten!

What is the name of this piece of artwork?
"Maple Syruped"

What inspired you to create this piece of art?
First of all, my family has tapped maples and cooked "homemade" maple syrup for decades. I love maple syrup. I witnessed the power of a young dark-eyed woman as she eyed her fiancé before and during a wedding ceremony.

I was overcome with the wonderful power of a woman to communicate so much transforming love in just a glance!

How do you see hope within your artwork?
The effect of a deep and sincere human love reminds me of God's great love in Christ –that we can be suddenly changed by another's love, freely and transparently given.

What is one Christian scripture that is connected to your art?

"You have stolen my heart, my sister, my bride; you have stolen my heart with one glance of your eyes, with one jewel of your necklace." Song of Songs 4:9 (NIV)

How do religion and culture influence your work?
At the same time of writing this verse, my wife and I were supervising and living in a co-ed Mission House we started on a Christian college campus (NWC-Iowa).

In building community, we would read weekly selections from Bonhoeffer's "Life Together", prepare meals from other cultures, and join for breakfast and prayer on Friday mornings and do service projects together.

During one of these breakfasts, the women students in the house remarked how "men are like waffles, all compartmentalized . . . Women are more like pancakes, when you put butter and syrup on it soaks into everything."

Food is often used to convey images of love across cultures. The vehicle of this particular kind of food seemed so appropriate for communicating with men and women the wonder that occurs when human beings let others love them; it transforms them, often sweetly and surprisingly!

French (English)
"Vous avez volé mon coeur, ma soeur, ma femme; Vous avez volé mon coeur avec un regard de vos yeux avec un bijou de votre collier." Cantique des Cantiques 4:09 (NIV) **Hope Translator: Erika Lobe (Baltimore, Maryland, USA)**

Love

66. Hope Artist Reflection: Oneness

English (Afrikaans)
Hope Artist: Jesse Versailles
Location: Sandy Point, Saint Kitts, West Indies

What is the name of this piece of artwork?
"Oneness"

What inspired you to create this piece of art?
I was inspired to create this piece because I was thinking about what true love should be. Oneness makes you so close with the person that you are with. It is as if you see, hear, and speak for each other. That's why the eyes, nose, and lips are one.

How do you see hope within your artwork?
I see hope in this piece because to be in love and to love is

worth it.

What is one Christian scripture that is connected to your art?

Adam and Eve inspired this piece. They seem to have had a great feel for one another in every way: spirit, mind, and body.

"And Adam called his wife's name Eve, because she was the mother of all living." – Genesis 3: 20 (NKJV)

How do religion and culture influence your work?

Religion and culture are about who you are inside. Therefore, it can't help but to come out naturally. My religion and culure show up in my art.

Afrikaans (English)

"En die mens het sy vrou Eva genoem, omdat sy moeder geword het van al wat lewe." Genesis 3:20 (Die Ganse Heilige Skrif Bible, 1940) **Hope Translator: Roxanne Van Wyk (Durban, South Africa)**

67. How to Love Your Bullies

English (Malayalam)

"But I tell you this: Love your enemies, and pray for those who persecute you. In this way you show that you are children of your Father in heaven." Matthew 5: 44-45 (GW)

When you've been bullied most of your life, you make a habit of blaming others for your low self-esteem. This is most certainly the case for me. Throughout my school years, my classmates would find a way to pick on everything about me.

In attempts to avoid being picked on, I would use other's opinions to gauge whether or not I was doing something right; for example, if I wasn't getting picked on, then my outfit must have been acceptable.

In the same way, I would blame others whenever my fragile self-confidence was broken by a rude comment or judging glare. I didn't realize it at the time, but I was building up a bitterness towards people.

This negative view towards others slowly grew with every hurtful remark made about me. Even as a college student studying abroad in New Zealand, I found myself overly affected by others' opinions of me. One night, I decided to go on a late-night grocery store run.

On my way to the store, I was passed by a car filled with a group of guys who, upon seeing me, yelled, "It's Whoopi! Hey, Whoopi!" All too familiar with the insulting tone of their remarks, I felt my thin confidence once again begin to shatter.

However, before the hurtful words could really sink in, a strong voice within me firmly declared, "No." It was the voice of God, a voice with which I had become increasingly familiar over the past month.

I had recently been praying for God to show me who I am meant to be in Him, and for Him to teach me how to build my confidence in Him. It is truly amazing how quickly God will answer your prayers when you diligently seek Him first.

God helped me to understand that I could no longer base my confidence in something as temporal as opinions; I had to place my confidence in Him. He further showed me that by placing my self-esteem on the opinions of others, I was hindering my ability to love them as Christ does. How could I fully love someone that I held responsible for my low self-confidence? I simply could not.

Upon realizing this, I immediately forgave every single one of my past bullies for their harsh words. I also asked God to forgive me for having a bitterness towards them, and for not loving them as purely as I should.

Through His word and His actions, Jesus teaches us to love those that aren't always easy to love. Putting my confidence in God allows me to purely love my bullies, and in doing so, I am living and loving more like Christ.

Hope Writer: Niya Tanyi (Los Angeles, California, USA)

Malayalam (English)
"Njano ningalodu parayunnathu; ningalude shakthrukkale snehikkuvin; ningale upadravikkunnavarkku vendi prarthikkuvin; Swargasthanaya ningalude pithavinu puthranmarai theerendathinu thanne; avan dhustanmarude melum nallavarude melum thante suryane udhippikkukayum neethimanmarude melum neethikettavarude melum mazha peyikkukayum cheyunnuvallo." *Mathai 5:44-45* **Hope Translator: Gladson Thomas (Kottayam, Kerala, India)**

68. Jesus' Patience Draws Us Back Unto His Divine Love

English (German)

I awarely divorced myself from the love of God when I was in my first year of high school. I was about 12 years of age. I wanted to be alone, totally independent from God's provision, guidance, and leadings on Earth.

I said, "God, I don't want to have anything to do with you anymore. Leave me alone. I don't need you. I can live without you."

I put my bible aside and never ever touched it again until 18 long years had passed. I forgot everything about God and lived on my own—all by myself, with my own human ways! In short, I did this and that; I went here and there – looking everywhere in the world for answers to many questions about life and its truth!

I did what I had to do diligently… studied and worked, hoping to find the way to happiness & contentment – to no avail. I became half atheist and half believer.

One Cold Christmas day in 1982, my husband-to-be in Europe invited me to attend church. I said to myself, "Okay, if my husband to be is a Catholic, then I will be a Catholic. If he is a Buddhist, I will be Buddhist; if he is a Baptist or Protestant, then I will be a Baptist or a Protestant. Whatever he is, I will be just like him. He is going to be my husband, anyway."

When we got in the fully-packed St. Niklaus church, I kneeled and talked to God mentally from my heart, in a whisper. To my surprise, a very clear, distinct voice answered – as if there were a microphone! "Even if you turned your back away from me, I love you just as you are."

It gripped my heart painfully into sobbing! For the very first time in my whole life, I wept – shedding tears of regret and shame with a loud cry! My shoulders were going up and down, touching my jaws, uttering, "God, forgive me! Everything I did was only for me and myself. You didn't have any part of it. It was only mine! Just me and mine! Please, forgive me!"

I went on catching my breath, weeping of repentance for having run away from Him. I shook off all of my sins unto God, penitently!

That was my very first encounter with the holy, loving, living God.

"I no longer live, but Christ lives in me. The life I now live I live by believing in God's Son, who loved me and took the punishment for my sins." –Galations 2:20 (GW)

Hope Writer: Lillith Maxilom Skrzpek (Kiel, Germany)

German (English)
"Nicht mehr ich lebe, sondern Christus lebt in mir. Soweit ich aber jetzt noch in dieser Welt lebe, lebe ich im Glauben an den Sohn Gottes, der mich geliebt und sich für mich hingegeben hat." Galater 2,20 (GW) **Hope Translator: Ha Feh (Kiel, Germany)**

69. Compassionate Warrior-ship

English (Sepedi)
"Teacher, I saw an accident yesterday, near our office. It was an old man and a woman. They had been hit by a car." My student described an incident she had witnessed in her home country of Myanmar.

It was a scene I could easily imagine. I had seen similar tragedies and, of course, heard of so many more like this one while living and working abroad.

"Teacher, I ran to where they were lying. There were many people standing around, but no one was helping them. Someone had called the ambulance, but they would not come unless someone promised to pay them . . . I shouted at the people for someone to help them, but no one would do anything. I cried so hard . . . it hurt in my heart so badly."

As these words – typed out from halfway around the world – appeared on my screen, I could feel my student's frustration, her heartbreak for the old couple – poor people from the countryside unexpectedly caught up in an unfortunate incident with no resources, friends or family available to help them. A scene, a situation, repeated innumerable times in countless places.

In another professional lifetime, as a hospice chaplain, I was a direct witness to the mental, physical, and spiritual suffering that often accompanies a terminal illness.

In my more recent work as a development and peace educator, I have been introduced to the kinds of suffering visited upon entire communities through poverty, lack of education, filthy living conditions, unfair social and political systems . . . you get the picture.

Like my student I, too, at times felt overwhelmed by the enormity of situations I knew I could do very little about. Being in the presence of intense suffering can cause you to want to withdraw, pull in, retract; it can break your heart.

In recent years, I have wanted to know and to learn how to be with people in situations that I find heartbreaking – without withdrawing, shutting down or distracting myself from the pain around me.

Just as importantly, I have wanted to learn how to "participate joyfully in the sorrows of the world." Easy to do? Not at all! Who can feel joyful or want to stay present and engaged when their heart is hurting and sad, when we've been abused?

In fact I would be foolish to not give myself some space, to protect myself from allowing further infliction of pain and abuse. Jesus' heart was continually hurt as he faced and lived amongst the ignorance, poverty, privation, cruelty, greed, and division that characterized his time.

The Gospel of John 11:35 "Jesus wept," gives the most terse and poignant evidence of Jesus' broken heart and of his compassion. And yet, Jesus doesn't weep with impotence, rather he "sets his face for Jerusalem" (Luke 9:51) and shows determined compassionate warrior-ship.

For me learning and practicing the idea of participating joyfully in the sorrows of the world is a lifelong vow, challenge, and spiritual experiment I am determined to complete. Noble words, I suppose. Words I need grace to live up to every day. Yet Jesus' example shows me that I can choose to remain open and present even with my pain right there for all to see; to try all along the way to not close down completely.

I can choose to allow my broken heart to become the womb of a deeper compassion – for myself and for my fellow strugglers, each walking his or her own path.

"And it came to pass, when the time was come that he should be received up, he steadfastly set his face to go to Jerusalem." – Luke 9:51 (KJV)

Hope Writer: Blakely Gooch (Yangon, Burma)

Sepedi (English)
"E rile ge nako ya gore Jesu a rotogele legodimong e batametše, a ikemišetša go ya Jerusalema gomme a wela tsela a ya gona." **Lukase 9:51 (KJV) Hope Translator: Warrel Stephen Mothoa (Soweto, South Africa)**

70. Yes Jesus Loves Me

English (Malayalam)
"Yes, Jesus loves me. Yes, Jesus loves me. Yes Jesus loves me, for the Bible tells me so." I learned that little phrase a child. I must have sung this song a thousand times.

It wasn't until I was at one of my lowest points that this song came alive, and in a new and inspiring way. We humans have something built in us that make us want love and affection from others.

In some cases, we struggle with hurt and pain because we

don't receive the love and affection from those that we expect to give it to us. We expect love, respect, and support from parents, spouses, significant others, family, and friends.

However, we live in a world where more people divorce than stay together, parents' problems keep them from being there for their kids, and friends let you down.

In the midst of these unfavorable circumstances, we can have hope based on the truth in a little childhood song. Yes, Jesus loves me.

Nothing can ever stop God from loving us. God's love is unconditional and it endures forever. Every day God proves, reaffirms, validates, verifies, and confirms His love for us.

During my dark time this song assured me that God's love was all I needed and that because of His love for me He would come to my rescue. He did . . . which gives me a reason and the right to sing, "Yes, Jesus loves me."

"For God so loved the world that He gave His only begotten Son, that whoever believes in Him should not perish but have everlasting life." John 3: 16 (NKJV)

Hope Writer: Dr. Adrian Manley (Clermont, Florida, USA)

Malayalam (English)
"Thante eekajathanaya puthranil viswasikkunna evanum nashichu pokathe nithya jeevan prapikkendathinu Daivam avane nalkuvan thakkavannam lokathe snehichu." Yohannan 3:16 (KJV) **Hope Translator: Gladson Thomas (Kottayam,**

Kerala, India)

71. Self-Worth is Worth Embracing!

English (French)
According to an on-line definition, self-worth is defined as respect for or a favorable opinion of oneself. Society has played a major role in how we view ourselves. Public media, social media, and personal experiences are influences that have affected our thinking of what and who we are "supposed" to be.

For some, the sense of "self" became distorted and maybe even quite confusing through family and certain socio-cultural upbringings. I have personally experienced times when I measured myself up with other women with better careers, relationships, physical attributes – and how they socialized with others. I used to feel as if I would never have that influence.

The point we miss is that, each of us experiences our own journey towards developing an unconditional love with ourselves. We aren't always privileged to see the struggle, roads traveled, and the obstacles crossed by others to have prospered or seem to have it all together. We may not know all they have endured and still be working towards to maintain that level of self-worth.

A few scriptures that helped me to grow and love me for me are *Romans 12:2, "Do not be conformed to this world, but be transformed by the renewal of your mind, that by testing you may discern what is the will of God, what is good and acceptable and perfect." (ESV)* The way we think and feel is a path towards learning and knowing who we are and is a process we must go through. The next scripture is what I say to God in thanks from *Psalm 139:13-15, "For you formed my inward parts; you knitted me together in my mother's womb. I praise you, for I am fearfully and wonderfully made. Wonderful are your works; my soul knows it very well. My frame was not hidden from you, when I was being made in secret, intricately woven in the depths of the earth." (ESV)*

I thank you, God, for creating me already with self-worth. We were all different on purpose; God's design!

I am finally in a place where I don't mind saying "no" if saying "yes" compromises how I feel about me. If I don't like something about me, I work on it; I think about why I think these things then focus towards changing for the better – for me.

With all this being written, I want to advise all reading this: know that YOU are a precious gift from GOD. Respect yourself and you will not let yourself be disrespected or mistreated by others.

Love yourself and do not allow yourself to be in relationships that are not healthy (male and female). See yourself as a precious gift that you just can't give to everybody! Make careful decisions and choices about who you share YOU with. You LIVE, you LOVE, and you LAUGH and find ways to enjoy YOUR life no matter what situation you are in.

Your self-worth is worth embracing!

Hope Writer: NaTisha Peacock (Greensboro, North Carolina, USA)

French (English)
"Pour vous formé mes organes; vous me tricoté dans le ventre de ma mère. Je te fais l'éloge, pour je suis fabrique craintivement et merveilleusement. Merveilleuses sont tes œuvres; mon âme le sait très bien. Mon corps n'était point caché devant toi, lorsque j'ai été fait dans le secret, tissé dans les profondeurs de la terre."
Psaume 139:13-15 (ESV) **Hope Translator: Erika Lobe (Baltimore, Maryland, USA)**

72. A Lesson Of Love Through Pain

English (Jamaican Patois)
About a year ago, I met a man overseas and fell in love. I realized he was broken – miserable, needy – and didn't know how to show love.

I'm not very patient, but I realized that he needed patience! The Holy Spirit instructed me to encourage and support him. But I would soon bear my grandmother's death, hospitalizations, bondage, and natural disasters. These required emotional, spiritual – and financial – support. I thought, "Run as far and as fast as you can."

How could I have fallen in love? I was pouring so much into him and not receiving a thing. Our relationship became one of him wanting and me giving.

There were times I wanted affection. But then he would be going through some issue – or just couldn't be found.

One time, after crying myself to sleep, I cried out to God. I had been asking the Lord to reveal His will. I wondered why God would reward my faithfulness with an overly needy, impassionate partner? I was listening to a song my friend wrote for his wife. He described God's unconditional love for His people.

I realized that God wanted me to love him – despite his many flaws. I became even more supportive and patient. This opened the door for a marriage proposal.

I accepted because I felt that this man needed me and I needed a man. Maybe I could love him enough to help him and we would both get what we wanted. Of course that's not how it works! But things weren't going how I thought they should. The disturbance in my spirit increased.

I realized I couldn't see myself going forward with someone without spiritual substance.

The more I got to know him, the more I realized that, while I could love him, I couldn't make him have a relationship with God. My happiness turned to tears. There was nothing here for me.

On one occasion, as I prayed, I was asking God, "Why is this happening to me?" It was then that it dawned on me. I had done the same thing to the Lover of My Soul! This is exactly how God felt when he wanted my attention and I refused him.

When we reject Christ, his heart hurts! I realized that My Lord was always there for me! He supplied my every need even when I didn't ask Him! He was patient with my frequent failings! Even when I had given my heart to another man, He loved me.

The relationship with this man has ended. This was my

lesson – to truly understand the pain, rejection, and suffering that comes from a one-sided love relationship. I thank the Lord for the privilege to learn this valuable lesson.

For the learning to take place there had to be pain. My acceptance of this truth and the study of God's Word are helping me to forgive and move past my pain. The process of recovery is not easy, but knowing that God has got me makes it so much easier. To God be all the Glory!

"Because of the Lord's great love we are not consumed, for his compassions never fail. They are new every morning; great is your faithfulness." Lamentations 3:22-23 (NIV)

Hope Writer: Dr. Stephanie Fletcher (Sydney, New South Wales, Australia)

Jamaican Patois (English)
"Me wahn yu fi noe seh a cause de Lawd luv big suh till, a dats why we nuh mash up an ded a'ready, cause fi him compasshan neva fail yet! Every mawning is a new set a compasshan; Massa Gad faithful nuff nuff." Lamentations 3:22-23 (NIV) **Hope Translator: Dr. Stephanie Fletcher (Sydney, New South Wales, Australia)**

73. Indescribable Grace

English (Spanish)
"My grace is sufficient for you, for my power is made perfect in weakness." 2 Corinthians 12:9 (NIV)

The Voices…

"You know little girls with no mama don't amount to anything." I ask, "Why not, Auntie?" The voice continues to say, "You ain't got no future. Ain't nobody gonna want anything to do with you." Heartbroken, I fearfully ponder, "I'm 14 years old. God, is this really true? Why, God? Please God, don't let it be true! Please! I want a future of love. I don't want to be alone. I'm scared!"

The Grace...

When I found myself feeling lonely, incompetent, and inadequate in my early teen years, I knew enough about the essence of God to feel free to petition for help. I did not rely upon my own abilities. Jesus made it very clear that, with Him, all things are possible.

I believed my needs would be met if I only asked. This was my youthful faith that has served me well into adulthood. Whatever you need in life, take it to God in prayer! By requesting and allowing God to work in and through me, I have achieved much success that would have otherwise been unattainable in my own strength.

This truth was the answer to all my fears, doubts, and insecurities. The real truth is . . . I always was a Love child and so are you! Mother Love has timeless grace . . . ready to be given, if only we will humbly ask. Hallelujah, I am loved and I am somebody!

God. I thank you and praise you for the wonderful assurance that I can do all things through Christ who strengthens me. Amen.

Hope Writer: Georgia Chambers (Houston, Texas, USA)

Spanish (English)
"Mi gracia es todo lo que necesitas; mi poder actúa mejor en la debilidad." *2 Corintios 12:9 (NIV)* **Hope Translator: Rebecca Holderman (Centralia, Washington, USA)**

74. Be Yourself

English (Haitian Creole)
With all the pressures and demands that life brings, walking around and trying to gain approval from everyone is the last thing I needed.

In this case, I have come to realize that there are three types of people: some you can please; some you'll sometimes please; and some you'll never please. All three cases have one thing in common and it is that you will never be able to please everyone at all times.

I believe that the three main hindrances for normal, genuine people to reveal their true self is that they sense a need to protect themselves from the fear of criticism, the fear of rejection or the fear of hurt.

Others may refer to people who are like this as being "thin skinned" or not "normal," but what I really see is people who have been through a lot in the past and need a little extra tender loving care to give them a "PUSH" in life.

With all that being said, if you know someone who needs to loosen up a bit, shower them with love and give them added assurance to help them make the steps needed. Or, if you are like this, you might as well remove your mask, let your hair down, loosen up a bit, take some risk – and live a little.

You will not have everyone's approval but you can guarantee, while some people won't always like you, there are some who will definitely love you. Instead of focusing on those who do not like you, draw from the ones who love you. That seems like the better choice to me. Be yourself; move past the negatives and embrace the love. Life is worth living!

"But the LORD said to Samuel, 'Don't judge by his appearance or height, for I have rejected him. The LORD doesn't see things the way you see them. People judge by outward appearance, but the LORD looks at the heart.'" 1 Samuel 16:7 (NLT)

Hope Writer: Author Terry-Ann Scott (Mandevile, Jamaica, West Indies)

Haitian Creole (English)
"Men, Seyè a di Samyèl:-'pa jije sou figi l' osinon wotè, Paske mwen mete l '. Seyè a pa wè bagay wout la ou wè yo. Moun ki jije sou figi deyò, men Seyè a parèt nan kè a. 1 Samuel 16:7 (NLT) **Hope Translator: Kirk Louis (Midwest City, Oklahoma, USA)**

75. Replenish Myself

English (Filipino)
I have found a very easy, yet very powerful way to replenish myself – my body and my spirit. It's something I learned while studying about self-empowerment – a kind of creative visualization, if you will. It's something we can all do to keep ourselves balanced and joyful and healthy. It

is completely "anti-stress" and will only allow positive energy to flow.

If you rely too heavily on sighing to keep from spontaneously combusting, or if you feel that your internal "tank" is way beyond empty, or if putting one foot in front of the other is like a major workout for you, do try this.

In a safe and quiet place (I use my bedroom floor or bed), get on your back. Intend to relax your muscles. Unclench your fists. Relax your face, your legs, your belly, everything – and then envision you are under a massive tree.

The tree is full of leaves and you can see the sun shining through those leaves. Then allow the leaves to softly start falling on you; see them as lights falling on you. The leaves fall one at a time at first – then they fall all over and around you, each one bringing you the light of self-worth – the light of an all-loving God.

Allow yourself time to feel the lights recharging your spirit. Whisper to yourself, "Thank you God. You love me so much. I love me too!" Slowly rise, lift your chin to the heavens, breathe in the very air that is a gift to you – and smile.

Now go make the world a better place!

"Come to Me, all you who labor and are heavy laden, and I will give you rest." Matthew 11: 28 (NKJV)

Hope Writer: Debbie Wallace Whittington-Robinson (Mebane, North Carolina, USA)

Filipino (English)

"Magsiparito sa akin, kayong lahat na nangapapagal at nangabibigatang lubha, at kayo'y aking papagpapahingahin."
Mateo 11: 28 **Hope Translator: Rose Canlas (Baguio City, Philippines)**

Solidarity and Justice

76. Oppression

English (Malayalam)
Sometimes I wonder, how many times can one's heart get
ripped out?
How many times can one's spirit get squeezed out?
How many times can one feel so beaten up, that the hope
of standing up is a dream – long lost in the distant
imaginary?

Sometimes the causes of oppression are hard to make
sense of. I was never taught the language.

Racism – they say we were just baked differently in God's
oven. So we judge from dark to light.
Gender – they use biology to describe our biological
capacities, our inabilities, the lack of our emotional
rationality.

Class – they say that it was our karma to be born into the
class that we have, and we must toil and labour so others
can profit.
Sexuality – they say stay within the bounds of the boxes
and exploration is a sin.
Body image – they say if you don't look like that Victoria
Secret angel, you are too ugly for love.
Nationality – there is no saying, often just evicting out of
place, shooting, and killing.
And Love – the kind you would sacrifice your life for. But
the kind, that is taught to hate because of gender, race,
nationality and class.

The multiple generations of women that have raised me,
have taught me to LOVE unconditionally and GIVE

unconditionally.
To do so is God's work.
But when unconditional love destroys your heart and
spirit – and has nothing to give in return – how can the
broken ever stand again?

Years have passed and the light sometimes shines in. The
light that says, "To think of yourself as small or little in
relation to your love, is disrespecting the divine."
The divine made us with love.
The divine crafted us with love: regardless of the shade of
our skins, the biology that marks us into genders, the
wealth that marks our value, the space that one is bound to
called the nation, and the body size that marks if we can be
loved.
If the divine loves you, then you not loving yourself – and
letting others rip your heart out, and squeeze your spirit,
and kill your self esteem – is disrespecting the divine.

Can one disrespect the divine?
What about unconditional love and conditional giving?
How do we honor our mother's teachings if we disrespect
the divine?
To stand tall, one can look deep within – and love oneself.
In loving oneself, you will see the divine.
And when one sees the divine, one will love and give the
divine within, unconditionally.
And with that one will see the light that gives strength to
stand.
Not just stand. But stand tall.

To heal.
Healing is respect for oneself, and respect for the divine.
Life's journeys will make us fall time and time again, bring

us trouble and grief.

Don't seek light on the outside, seek it inside.

The divine is there.

When you see her/him, you will awaken.

You will heal.

"But he's already made it plain how to live, what to do, what GOD is looking for in men and women. It's quite simple: Do what is fair and just to your neighbor, be compassionate and loyal in your love, And don't take yourself too seriously — take God seriously." Micah 6: 8 (MSG)

Hope Writer: Anonymous, A Well Wisher

Malayalam (English)

"Manukshya, Nallathu enthennu avan ninakku kanichu thannirikkunnu.: nyam pravarthikkuvanum dheya thalparanairikkuvanum ninte Daivathinte Sannidhiyil thazhmayode nadakkuvanum allathe enthakunnu Yehova ninnodu chodikkunnathu?" Meekha 6: 8 (MSG) **Hope Translator: Gladson Thomas (Kottayam, Kerala, India)**

77. Going Against The Norm Has Proven To Be Beneficial

English (Spanish)

I am a member of the AMEC. AMEC means African Methodist Episcopal Church. We are Methodist and we have a "method" of doing things. According to Webster's Dictionary, the word method means a systematic procedure; orderliness in manner or mode.

There are 3 people who did great things, but had to go

outside of the norm in order to do so. Bishop Richard Allen, who founded the AME Church went outside the box by working hard and buying a blacksmith shop, turning that shop into our first AME Church. Now we have churches all over – from the United States to Africa.

The 2nd person that comes to mind is Moses. His life was abnormal from the very beginning because he was a Hebrew raised as an Egyptian. The Lord placed him as an Egyptian to do the Lord's will, but Moses had to go through some things first. For all that Moses did we will never forget him – or his contributions to history!

Lastly Paul, the Apostle. God used Paul by allowing him to go against his own people. He was Hebrew with Roman heritage, but God allowed him to be exposed to all things and all people so that he would be a great witness of God's power. So the person who ended up persecuting people ended up being a prisoner for Christ! What was unique about Paul was that he wasn't in the upper room with the other apostles – yet he became a great apostle, and wrote two-thirds of the New Testament.

There is strength in the name of Jesus! For strength, read *Psalms 28:7, "The LORD is my strength and my shield; my heart trusted in him, and I am helped: therefore my heart greatly rejoiceth; and with my song will I praise him." (KJV)*

Now that it's a new year, maybe it's time to do things differently for some things that we want to happen for the greater good!

Hope Writer: Kerri Rigsbee (Kannapolis, North Carolina, USA)

Spanish (English)

"El Senor es mi fuerza y mi escudo; en El confía mi corazón, y soy socorrido; por tanto, mi corazón se regocija, y le daré gracias con mi cántico." Salmos 28:7 (KJV) **Hope Translator: Rebecca Holderman (Centralia, Washington, USA)**

78. Women and Shoes

English (Filipino)
What is it with women and shoes? A pair of shoes can make a difference to an arduous journey (a mountain trekker comes to mind). For some, it becomes a status symbol (Louboutins, Nike) or something to perk your gloomy day.

A comfortable pair of footwear would be your best partner for a life-long journey, literally. For more than two hundred workers – the majority of whom are women who produce Philippine brand Advan Shoes – it spells a huge difference between daily survival and abject poverty.

Advan Shoes, since its establishment in 1990, has become a lucrative business owned by a Filipino-Chinese businessman. In the face of stiff competition – both from domestic and imported goods of casual shoes and rain boots, Advan Shoes continue to gain market share and supplying the biggest chain of malls in the country.

The workers estimated the recent production output of rain boots at 2,700 pairs per day and the shoes at 5,400 pair per day. From January 2012 to February 2013, estimated total sales amounts to P95.7 million or nearly USD2.4 million from 407,550 pairs. Ironically, very few workers own a pair as it takes a backseat over food and education.

Indeed, producing Advan Shoes has never been a walk in the park. On the afternoon of May 18, 2013, I saw women – mothers, workers, labor leaders – not on their workstations but outside the manufacturing site standing ground as they held their picket lines.

It was the height of their struggle against inhumane treatment, low and delayed salaries, sexual harassment, union busting and violations to the collective bargaining agreement that has spanned for more than two decades now. Currently, they have been forcibly imposed with a forced leave and no-work policy on the ground of heavy indebtedness – a reason largely questionable, as the company continues to produce based on market demand despite a rotational work schedule.

The people who breathe life and development not only to a company – but more importantly, to a nation – are bleeding dry from wretched poverty and intense starvation. In a country where the minimum wage is a far cry from the family living wage, any disruption in the economic life (labor contractualization, rotational work schedule, job insecurity, price increase of basic commodities) is a heavy burden to the whole family.

But instead of agreeing to the inhumane labor practices of the company just to sustain employment, workers joined the picket lines to assert their labor rights and reclaim dignity.

A makeshift sari-sari store (small convenience store) was put up to generate income and sustain their struggle.

Mothers take turns in attending to the children. Others take temporary jobs to meet the needs of the fellow workers at the picket line.

Hope springs eternal as they sustain the battle amidst odds of economic hardships and family demands. The clamor never ceases – so that workers, at their full potential, can benefit from the fruits of their labor and their handiwork as a continuing act of creation regarded with dignity and honor. And then, most probably, we can find a pair or two of Advan Shoes in the homes of workers.

"And hope does not disappoint us, because God has poured out his love into our hearts by the Holy Spirit, whom he has given us." Romans 5:5 (NIV)

Hope Writer: Iris Ann Agustin-Capus (Quezon City, Phiilippines)

Filipino (English)
"At ang pagasa ay hindi humihiya; sapagka't ang pagibig ng Dios ay nabubuhos sa ating mga puso sa pamamagitan ng Espiritu Santo na ibinigay sa atin." Mga Taga Roma 5:5 (NIV)
Hope Translator: Rose Renie Canlas (Baguio City, Philippines)

79. Counting on the Blessings: Target 1000 Packages for Relief

English (Filipino)
The day before the Relief Operations in the Philippines, we were still lacking 1,228 cans of sardines, 98 kilos of dried fish, 61.5 kilos of sugar, 27 kilos of mongo, and 529 500ml

bottles of cooking oil. Adding in the commitment from individuals and institutions, we still needed more resources.

By claiming what we commonly call the "faith" in us, strongly impelling us to believe – not a magic or paranormal source of belief, but a solid conviction that churches and many of us still have access to – we can appeal to potential givers and those whose hearts are ever generous. The truth remains that we just have to tap the innate capacity of human beings to be channels of blessings and services.

The counting of packages, and all the stuff needed to complete a bag of goodies, was meticulously done. Every gram matters and all those donated needed to be recounted, repacked – to complete the set. People are waiting out there. They do not know us. We do not know them. The tie that binds us together is disaster and challenges how we minister to one another. Blessings and commitment come.

At around minutes before 6 PM, we were given a go signal that the commitment to share would be ready by the week. That evening we had to make a loan from friends here and there. As it was Sunday, banks were closed – and transaction was not easy. Finally, at 9 PM we were able to finish the target packages – 1,000 bags of relief goodies.

We were able to come out with funds needed, with less than a P10,000.00 loan remaining. The amount was not too big to raise – as we still claimed that there would be a generous one who would share.

At 4 AM volunteers were up. At 6 AM we started to load the goodies packed with compassion and love. We finally reached the three communities in Laguna. It was a feeling of both heart-wretchedness and resolve – on the urgency for meaningful change.

In Binan, there were communities still under knee-high water for more than 20 days. People had to line up, patiently waiting for the relief goodies to be distributed.

They were so disciplined; the tickets that would assure them of packages were kept and guarded. Some tickets that got wet were placed in little plastic bags. Men, women, old and young alike queued for the goodies; dared the flood (that is certainly dirty and got the smell as anyone would imagine it); and humbly received those gifts – almost bowing their heads in appreciation.

Some were barefooted; others were not strong enough to carry the package; some were so tiny that their bare bones revealed the health situation of the community. A total of 1,000 bags were distributed. That is only a tiny fraction of 16,500 families affected.

We mobilized the resources – and the generosity of the people and organizations are testimony of great compassion.

"And I have been a constant example of how you can help those in need by working hard. You should remember the words of the Lord Jesus: 'It is more blessed to give than to receive.'" Acts 20: 35 (NLT)

Hope Writer: Norma P. Dollaga (Manila, Phillipines)

Filipino (English)

"Nagbigay halimbawa ako sa inyo sa lahat ng mga bagay, na sa ganitong pagpapagal ay dapat kayong magsisaklolo sa mahihina, at alalahanin ang mga salita ng Panginoong Jesus, na siya rin ang may sabi, Lalo pang mapalad ang magbigay kay sa tumanggap." Mga Gawa 20: 35 **Hope Translator: Rose Renie Canlas (Baguio City, Philippines)**

80. Jesus of The Liminals

English (Malayalam)

I'm an in-between girl. I'm half Indian and half Scottish. I'm the child of immigrants and an immigrant, but also American. I pastor a predominantly people-of-color church in a 92% white denomination, which is also a pro-gay, lesbian, bisexual, transgender, and questioning (GLBTQ) congregation in the midst of a lot of people-of-color churches that are very much not pro-GLBTQ.

The thing about being an in-between girl is that I often feel caught between communities I love who do not love each other very much. My denomination's caught in a debate over whether to publicly claim that it supports gay and lesbian ordination.

I watch people and communities I love being somewhat unloving to one another as they wrestle with this issue – and it breaks my heart. For us in-between people, debates that pit one group against another can leave us confused, frustrated or very, very lonely.

And then I think about Jesus, the king of the liminals. Liminal is a fancy word that means "1: of or relating to a sensory threshold; 2: barely perceptible; 3: of, relating to, or being an intermediate state, phase, or condition: in-between, transitional." I love that word, and it captures where Jesus spent his ministry.

I think about Jesus loving people in power and calling them into relationship with people who had no power. I think about Jesus hanging out with prominent religious leaders and inviting them into relationship with a woman they saw as dirty, fallen and beneath them.

I think about Jesus visiting Mary and Martha's home and encouraging a woman (a woman!) to sit at his feet and study and learn. Jesus lived in an in-between space all the time, and from that space, he showed that it is possible to radiate deep compassion in every direction.

The Latin root of liminal is "limin" or "threshold." How appropriate that this not either-or place – this in-between place – is also the threshold. Because Jesus also leads us to the threshold of revelation, the threshold of a whole new way of being, a way totally different than the brokenness of the world around us right now. Salvation is also being unmired from what is – and discovering what can be.

As I reflect on Jesus, my king, king of liminality, I realize that this in-between place is a holy place, a place of healing, a place of joy. And I feel grateful to be in relation with communities that do not yet realize that they will receive such a great gift from being united by Jesus, their king, king of liminality.

"Beloved, let us love one another: for love is of God; and every one that loveth is born of God, and knoweth God." 1 John 4: 7

(KJV)

Hope Writer: Sandhya Rani Jha (Oakland, California, USA)

Malayalam (English)
"Oru Shamarya sthree vellam koruvan vannu; Yesu avalodu ;enikku kudikkuvan tharumo ennu chodichu." 1 *Yohannan* 4: 7 (KJV) **Hope Translator: Gladson Thomas (Kottayam, Kerala, India)**

81. Bearing Witness to the Beating Hearts Before Us

English (Haitian Creole)
She was standing at the intersection, eyes darkened and stooped posture, barely just bones and flesh, her sign pleading for help: "Just some change." I wondered what she was ravished by: drugs? alcohol? a bad relationship? a sudden tragedy? circumstances beyond her control?

My heart ached. I pulled over and came up to her... her eyes meeting mine with hesitation and yet desperation. "Are you okay?" I asked. She answered with a halfhearted laugh and said, "Well, I am making by . . . I have a tent down by the tracks."

I knew the emptiness of words, my inability to fathom her state.. and yet.. my heart.. it ached, needing to respond. I reached out my hands to her and hugged her. She held me back. Goosebumps were shooting up and down my spine; her frail stature was trembling.

We stood this way for a moment, time standing still as cars

passed, people moving about their day.

She whispered, "You've been here before? You know?"

"Not exactly," I said, "but I think I understand. Are you safe?" I asked.

She looked at me cringing, her answer in her eyes.

"Pray to the Father. He will protect you," I said.

Her eyes searched me, clinging to any reassurance. I repeated firmly, "He will protect you. Pray to Him." She nodded . . . a bit calmed.

I handed her the small amount of money I had brought with me that day and walked back to my car – wanting to do more and yet at a loss of what else to do.

My daughter sat waiting in her car seat. "Is she okay, Momma?" she innocently asked.

"I hope so hunny," I answered.

I never saw her again. I think of her though. Every time I see a woman with a sign on the roadside, I pause and peer to find that face. I say a little prayer for her. It does not feel like much, but it is all I have to offer her.

There are so many beating hearts before us. So many lost in sin, oppression, and the powers of darkness. So much pain and loss. So much need.

So how do we reconcile to our faith, the Kingdom that is to come?

Look at the beating hearts before you. Nurse the afflicted. Weep with them. Cry out to our savior. Plead their case. Offer compassion. Offer yourself... as a witness, as a testimony, as a hope. Feel with them – in their pain, in their loss, in their desperation.

Offer your heart. Offer God's Love.

Be assured:

"For I was hungred, and ye gave me meat: I was thirsty, and ye gave me drink: I was a stranger, and ye took me in: Naked, and ye clothed me, I was sick, and ye visited me: I was in prison, and ye came unto me... Inasmuch as ye have done it unto one of the least of these my brethren, ye have done it unto me." Matthew 25: 35, 36, 40b (KJV)

Hope Writer: Jasmine Joy Landry (High Rolls, New Mexico, USA)

Haitian Creole (English)
"Pou mwen te grangou, nou ban m 'manje, mwen te swaf dlo, nou ban m' bwè: Mwen te lwen peyi, nou te pran m 'nan: toutouni, nou ban m' rad, Mwen te malad, nou pran swen m ': Mwen te nan prizon, nou vin wè mwen... chak fwa nou te fè sa pou yonn nan pi piti pami frè m ', nou te fè sa pou mwen." Matye 25: 35, 36, 40b (KJV) **Hope Translator: Kirk Louis (Midwest City, Oklahoma, USA)**

82. Hope Artist Reflection: Sa Iyo Mahal kong Anak (My Dear Daughter)

English (Filipino)
Hope Artist/Hope Writer: Norma P. Dollaga
Location: Manila, Phillipines

(Imagining Nanay Linda Cadapan, mother Sherlyn and Nanay Concepcion Empeño, mother of Karen. They are students of UP who were abducted on the 26th of June 2006.)

Until when is the search?
Must eternity wait?
I hope you would not be offended
That even if I search many precincts
And visit hundreds of tombs
Our path has never met yet
Countless times I search for you, every single second I look for you
I apologize that even in your suffering, I could not give you my warmest embrace

Where are you my daughter
Is it cold there?
Have they taken your wits
Have they broken your bones
And feasted over your skeleton?

Who are listening to your screams?
Have they wrecked your will?
Have they shattered your determination?

I am looking for you at all times

Just like you
I wish to be by your side

You must know, I have imbibed your courage
Never must your abductors think
That they could separate us by your conviction
Just like you, I have learned so many things
Like how to fight
Be strong my daughter

What is the name of this poem?
"Sa Iyo Mahal kong Anak (My Dear Daughter)"

What inspired you to create this poem?
I have met the mothers a couple of times—as they search and search for their daughters who were abducted while living with the farmers. First, they were searching for their own daughters, then they were co-searching with the parents and loved ones of those who were abducted and have disappeared.

They search for justice. They find commonality in the angry, sacred, loving search for those whose lives are offered for the sake of others. They are now part of an organization called Desaparasidos.

How do you see hope within your poem?
This can spread the hope inspired by these mothers. Usually we hear the children saying, "We will continue what our parents have started," Now, I hear them say, "We will continue the work of our daughters we valued and cherished most."

What is one Christian scripture that is connected to your poem?

"Can a woman forget her nursing-child, or show no compassion for the son of her womb? Even these may forget, yet I will not forget you." Isaiah 49: 15 (ESV)

How do religion and culture influence your work?

Culture did not come from a vacuum. Religious and art expressions mirror well a very particular perspective that comes from daily experiences, thus molding my viewpoint in life. Religious and faith expression connect myself to the reality of people's struggle. Hope nourishes my ministry and work.

Filipino (English)

"Malilimot ba ng ina ang kanyang pasusuhin, at hindi maaawa sa anak ng kanyang sinapupunan? Oo ,maaari nga, subalit hindi kita malilimutan." Isaya 49:15 (Biblia ng Sambayanang Pilipino) **Hope Translator: Norma P. Dollaga (Manila, Phillipines)**

83. Called To Be Peacemakers

English (Xhosa)

He who dwells in the shelter of the Most High will rest in the shadow of the Almighty.

I will say of the Lord, *"He is my refuge and my fortress my God, in whom I trust,"* says the Psalmist in Psalm 91:2 (KJV). The Bible also says, *"We are God's workmanship, created in Christ Jesus to do good works, which God prepared in advance for us to do."* – Ephesians 2:10 (NIV)

In one of the eight Beatitudes, Christ states, *"Blessed are the peacemakers, for they shall be called the children of God."* – *Matthew 5: 9 (KJV)* Peace as we usually refer to it – is shalom in Hebrew, meaning peace with justice – seems to be at the heart of Jesus' ministry recorded in the New Testament. Yet, peace is still a challenge in Africa.

It is still a challenge to hope that we are on a successful path to peaceful societies. The recurrent political instabilities in North, West, and Central Africa are becoming increasingly worrying.

African Christians and Churches may still be encouraged by certainty such as that of the Psalmist. In our struggles – however small the ways there may be to make peace with justice – we can be encouraged to carry on our Christian calling and duty to make peace with justice; because we serve the Most High.

Hope Writer: Marceline Niwenshuti (Pietermaritzburg, South Africa)

Xhosa (English)
"Banoyolo abaxolisi; ngokuba baya kubizwa ngokuthi bangoonyana bakaThixo bona." *Mathew 5:9 (KJV)* **Hope Translator: Sivu Twyabi (Johanessburg, South Africa)**

Discipleship

84. When Christianity Is Not Like Christ

English (Malayalam)
All I wanted to do was show her the crazy outfits in the 1960s section of the Oakland Museum. Seriously – I was just trying to make a bee line to the tie dye and the "Heck No We Won't Go" posters. But a teachable moment messed with my head instead.

My 9-year-old niece was visiting me from Holland, Michigan, where I joke with her father that he, his mother and his daughter make up one-third of the African American population. "Send her to me so she can see that the world is still a safe place even when she's in the majority," I said, and now we were visiting Ethiopian restaurants and Chinatown and going out for Indian food.

I even took her to a protest. She was terrified of getting arrested or not being allowed back in her favorite fast food place because of the "Subway is unfair" signs the picketers carried.

So for a lighter event, I took her to the museum, and headed towards the history section. Off to the left was a kayak woven from reeds and I thought, "We should talk about the fact that this land belonged to God and was lived on by the Ohlone Indians!" We talked about Native Americans and looked at artifacts.

She remembered me saying this was my favorite part of the museum and as she rounded the corner, she asked, "Is it your favorite because it's Christian?" I joined her and saw the cross of the Spanish conquistadores who claimed this state as theirs, in the name of Jesus Christ.

My niece is 9 and doesn't understand systemic oppression or colonization. Right now in her world there are nice people and not nice people, kind people and very bad people. There are not systems.

My niece's dad and I are both ministers. Of course my niece sees a cross and thinks that's what I like. But it attaches me to an ugly and unjust history where people did awful things and say that Jesus likes it, even though he doesn't.

I live in a town where a lot of people have given up on the church because it has judged and hurt them and ignored their needs and their voice. They hear Christian and associate it with bad things – they want nothing to do with it. But my nine-year-old niece doesn't know about any of that yet.

So I looked at the cross and said, "The Native Americans lived on this land. The Spanish came and took it away. That was wrong. Sometimes Christians do things that make Jesus Christ sad. And it makes him even more sad when they say they did it because of him."

And her response reminded me of how the gospel of Jesus Christ survives in the face of how often it is misused. She looked at me and said, "Oh! Like Hitler." And went on to look at all the Spanish artifacts.

A nine-year-old like my niece knows that Jesus is about love and about treating people nicely and about feeding the homeless (this is one that matters to her a LOT). She understands that people do awful things and say it's Jesus' will, but it's not.

To her, the conquistadores and Hitler and slave owners are not Christianity. My week with my niece reminds me that I want to be a Christian the way she defines a Christian, and if we all are, the world will be a lot more like the realm of God.

"But God is so rich in mercy, and he loved us so much." *Ephesians 2:4 (NLT)*

Hope Writer: Sandhya Rani Jha (Oakland, California, USA)

Malayalam (English)
"Karuna sambannanaya Daivamo namme snehicha maha sneham nimitham." Ephesiayer 2:4 (NLT) **Hope Translator: Gladson Thomas (Kottayam, Kerala, India)**

85. Hope Artist Reflection: The Parable of the Fish

English (French)
A man was in his row-boat, fishing with a rod and reel. As he caught each fish, he would throw it into the boat where a pile of them were flopping around and dying. One of the fish realized that she did not want to die, and that she must change to survive. "As things always change" the fish thought, "So must I change now." As this fish was contemplating the possibility of change, she could feel her gills were becoming able to breath the air.

She began speaking to her fellow fish saying. "You do not have to die, you have within you the ability to change and live; look, I have done it." One of the other fish listened to her and was convinced – he, too began breathing the air and spoke to other fish who also began changing. The fisherman turned his head and noticed something happening with the fish that he did not understand, so he grabbed an oar to beat them to death. As he raised up the oar one of the fish looked at him and said, "You do not have to kill us, for as we have changed to live in the air, so you may also change and live in the spirit of God."

What is the name of this piece of artwork?
"Parable of the Fish"

What inspired you to create this piece of art?
The parables of Jesus.

How do you see hope within your artwork?
We can all grow, change, repent, and live up to the challenges we face.

What is one Christian scripture that is connected to your art?
"Therefore if any man is in Christ, he is a new creature; the old things passed away; behold, new things have come." 2 Corinthians 5:17 (NASB 77)

How do religion and culture influence your work?
Religion influences my work by providing a relationship with the spirit; from this relationship flows the inspiration to create.

Hope Artist: Kent Forbes (Castine, Maine, USA)

French (English)
"Donc, si quelqu'un est en Christ, il est une nouvelle créature; les choses anciennes sont passes, voici, nouvelles choses sont venues." 2 Corinthiens 5:17 (NASB 77) **Hope Translator:**

Erika Lobe (Baltimore, Maryland, USA)

86. Pilgrim Notes: Shepherd

English (French)
Notes from a Five Month Bicycle Journey

"He had no beauty or majesty to attract us to him…" Isaiah 53:2
(NIV)

Biking through northern Greece we don't see many people
– mostly shepherds and their flocks. Actually, we keep a
wary eye out for sheep dogs, as they can be a bit
aggressive to bikers on the road. Often the shepherd is
there, however, and is able to call the dogs back if
necessary. It's the shepherd that strikes me.

It's the dissonance of the image of Shepherd in my mind
with what I see. In my subconscious, a shepherd is a
young, ruddy youth in white robes, sitting casually on a
rock with his shepherd's staff nearby, gazing out over
green pastures. Or a spotless Jesus with his usual Jesus
robes cradling a white-as-Christmas lamb that sleeps in his
arms.

In contrast, the image that is with me from three days ago
is an old man in dark and dirty clothes walking slowly
among a flock of goats, blowing smoke from his cigarette.
He had a small willow switch and his complexion was
dark and weathered. What strikes me most I think is that
this shepherd looked old and tired, slowly determined,
and dirty. He looked poor and old and homeless.

And there's the smell too – the smell of goats. When we're coming around a mountain road on our tandem, I can often be on the alert for the presence of sheep dogs by the wafting goaty smell – strong and warm and slightly acrid with a hint of manure. You can't spend all day with sheep or goats and not smell sheepy or goaty. It's a smell I would personally avoid. I prefer the smell of Herbal Essences and freshly-laundered clothing.

The point is all these things this shepherd was – old, tired, dirty, poor, smelly, alone – these are all offensive things. If not directly offensive, then subconsciously offensive – something we might pity or seek to ameliorate if one of our family members was so afflicted.

And then I snuggle down in my sleeping bag in our tent on some open patch of sheep grass next to an icy cold stream in which we hurriedly bathed, and I begin to pray: "The Lord is my shepherd...
he makes me lie down in green pastures
he leads me beside the quiet waters..."

O Lord, give us a fresh vision of yourself so that we may learn to identify with the likes of you.

Hope Writer: Andrew Spidahl (Holland, Michigan, USA)

French (English)
"il n'avait ni beauté, ni éclat pour que nous soyons attirés vers lui..." *Ésaïe 53:2* **Hope Translator: Andrew Spidahl (Holland, Michigan, USA)**

87. Loving and Forgiving Our Enemies

English (German)
I had a love-hate relationship with my Mom. I am a replica of her, but she – sort of – didn't like me. Being yelled at was normal! In my teens, I hated her more terribly because of serious family issues. Then God extraordinarily helped me with an intensive learning – under the Holy Spirit's guidance and leading.

It was hard for me to obey and follow the "Lord's command to forgive and love" my mother. One day, I asked God to help me in this area. Unexpectedly, Bill and Sandy, who had given up their millions for Jesus – came purposely from England to visit and minister to me here in Germany! In short, Sandy said, "You are saved now. You must forgive your mother as God forgave you."

I said, "Sandy, I'd like to forgive her! But I can't! I can't!" Sandy guided me in prayer: "Lord God, help me to forgive my Mom. I can't do it without Your strength in me."

God helped me forgive. That very night in July of 1985, I wrote a letter to my mother in the Phillipines telling her I had forgiven her heartily in Jesus' name. Two years later, in 1987, my Mom with my whole family – including my nephews and nieces, 21 in all – gave and surrendered their lives to Jesus when God sent me for the very first time on vacation back home to the Philippines.

Which commandment is the most important of all? In *Mark 12:29-31*, Jesus says, *"The most important is, 'Listen, Israel, the Lord our God is the only Lord. So love the Lord your God with all your heart, with all your soul, with all your mind, and with all your strength.' The second most important commandment is this: 'Love your neighbor as you love yourself.' No other commandment is greater than these."* (GW)

Jesus also taught us to love and forgive our enemies. We can now forgive because of God's power of love within us.

Hope Writer: Adelita V. Maxilom Skrzypek (Kiel, Germany)

German (English)

"Jesus antwortete: Das erste ist: Höre, Israel, der Herr, unser Gott, ist der einzige Herr. Darum sollst du den Herrn, deinen Gott, lieben mit ganzem Herzen und ganzer Seele, mit all deinen Gedanken und all deiner Kraft. Als zweites kommt hinzu: Du sollst deinen Nächsten lieben wie dich selbst. Kein anderes Gebot ist größer als diese beiden." Matthew 12, 29- 31 (GW) **Hope Translator: Ha Feh (Kiel, Germany)**

88. Be Ye Imitators of Christ!

English (Sepedi)

I spent most of my time sad and disappointed by people – feeling lonely and angry at people for things they didn't know they did. That period of being lonely was God's way of getting me alone. Because when you're alone, you have more time to meditate on his word, praise, and worship – and to hear what he has to say about your life.

I learnt a lot in a short space of time. One lesson God wants to perfect in all of us is to be imitators of Christ. From the beginning of time God wanted us to be like him; hence, he said to God the spirit and God the son: "Let us make a person in our image."

He started with saying to me that, "I want you to learn to worship in spirit and in truth, from the depth of your heart no matter the situation you're facing, because if you can do this, then you learn to connect your physical self to your spiritual man. Learn not to attach your happiness to material things so that you can fully enjoy the Joy of the Lord without limits – because nothing and nobody can take that away from you. For even though happiness is a fleeting emotion – and emotions are roller coasters that fluctuate with changing circumstances – believing that God is in control gives you the confidence to choose a positive attitude toward whatever happens."

Now that I've learnt all of this I get to know God better every day. Now I understand that I am not perfect, but God loves me either way – so why can't I show love to those who hurt me, because that's what the Bible teaches me.

Matthew 6:12 says, when we pray we should say *"forgive us our debts, as we also have forgiven our debtors."* (NIV) So God goes on to say I forgive; you must also forgive.

Finally we know that God hates selfishness. *Philippians 2:3 reads:: "Do nothing out of selfish ambition or vain conceit."* (NIV) God loves humility and kindness.

Job 6:14 notes, "Anyone who withholds kindness from a friend forsakes the fear of the Almighty." (NIV) Before we judge or get angry or respond to a person in a rude way we must think of how it will sit with them, put ourselves in their shoes no matter what they first did or said to us.

We must consider that some people act the way they do because they're going through tough times. We need to be kind, for everyone we meet is fighting some kind of battle. Take the opportunity to put a smile on your face and a kind word in your mouth and share the love of God to someone who needs it more than you know! That's what Jesus would do. Now, therefore, be ye imitators of Christ!

Hope Writer: Paseka Khosa (Johannesburg, South Africa)

Sepedi (English)
Jobo 6:14, "Mang kapa mang yo a kutlelago botho go mogwera wa gagwe o bontšha go se hlophe Modimo." (NIV) **Hope Translator: Warrel Stephen Mothoa (Soweto, South Africa)**

89. The Shoes Off My Feet

English (Spanish)
One day I was out walking around an area called City Lake in Rocky Mount, North Carolina. As I continued my walk, I noticed a man who was walking around the lake as well. When I approached him, I noticed that he was walking with socks on his feet that had been layered to form shoes.

I immediately looked around to see if anyone else had noticed this man, but it appeared that everyone else was just having a good time and enjoying the moment.

I began to ask God, "Lord, are we really that selfish? Do we ignore others who are in need? Do we complain – when others would love to trade places with us? Are we really that ungrateful? Lord, this can't be happening."

God replied, "Yes, but you don't have to be like everyone else. You have a choice at this moment to make an impact and difference in another person's life. Don't worry about what they are doing. Just do your part. Son, in *Acts 20:35*, I have reminded you: '*In everything I did, I showed you that by this kind of hard work we must help the weak, remembering the words the Lord Jesus himself said: 'It is more blessed to give than to receive.'*" (NIV)

So I immediately started slipping off the shoes that I had on my feet. I remembered spending around $160 on those shoes, and I was so happy to bless someone else with them. God spoke again, "Son, put your shoes back on your feet. Run to your car. In your trunk are a pair of brown loafers that will be more comfortable for him. Give him those."

I immediately made it back to my car to find the brown loafers – a pair of shoes I had only worn about two times. I made it back to the gentleman and introduced myself. "How are you, Sir? My name is Dameian, and I wanted to give you a pair of shoes to put on your feet because it is so cold out here." He hugged me and said, "Thanks so much, my brother." He tried the shoes on, and they were a perfect fit. I almost cried!

He said, "I am used to the cold, and I have been living like this so long that my feet are used to it; however, these shoes feel really great to my feet." I told him to be blessed and to keep the faith. I even told him that I appreciate God allowing me to see him that day. I continued, "Sir, your spirit has completely given me another outlook on life."

We hugged each other again. I walked away and made it to my car. When I turned around, he was gone.

I share this story as a reminder to be a blessing unto others. You never know when you are entertaining an angel *(Hebrews 13:2)*. I realized that day God was allowing me to be tested. He wanted to see if I would really do the things I have prayed to Him in private about.

After coming to an overall conclusion, I finally realized that the other people at the Lake were blinded; it wasn't meant for them to see the man in need. God was simply testing me. Lord, thank you for testing my heart and my spirit.

Hope Writer: Pastor Dameian Battle, MBA (Rocky Mount, North Carolina, USA)

Spanish (English)
"Con mi ejemplo les he mostrado que es preciso trabajar duro para ayudar a los necesitados, recordando las palabras del Señor Jesús: 'Hay más dicha en dar que en recibir.'" Hechos 20:35 (*NVI)* **Hope Translator: Rebecca Holderman (Centralia, Washington, USA)**

90. Be Careful What You Think

English (Haitian Creole)
Are you familiar with the popular Bible verse which says, "Whatsoever a man sow that shall he reap?" Or the famous saying, "What goes around comes around?" Quite often, we recognize the harsh effects our words and actions can have on us, while sometimes, we overlook

them. Another quote I agree with is, "be careful what you wish for," and I'll add – "because wishes can come true."

You know those days in the morning where you wish the alarm clock did not have to go off? Those moments when you wish you could just draw the sheets, lie in bed all day and do nothing, and the thought – or something close – comes to your mind: "I wish I had the flu." Or, "I wish I was sick so I don't have to report to work."

Maybe you even faked being sick or having so-called "emergencies" a few times! If you know you've been guilty, well, it's time to start watching what you think because it will come into reality sooner or later.

I recall a time in my life where I was fed up and ready to give up on life and everyone around me. Things were not working out for me and the Devil capitalized on my situation – and I bought into his lies.

Each morning I woke up, I was so depressed for the fact that I had life and I kept envisioning myself as intensely sick and dying. I wanted to get out of this world so badly that every core and fiber of my being felt what I envisioned and guess what? I became ill!

I was so sick to the point where I could not walk due to chronic back pain. I had to get shots at the hospital weekly for the severe pain I felt, which were no help to me. After spending a fortune on all sorts of tests, I was told I had a huge kidney stone that looked like a rock. The doctor sent me for another test before scheduling surgery. He said I needed to break the stone into pieces to get them out.

Well, guess what? During the same time, the Lord spoke to

me! He taught me a few lessons I will not share now; but one question he asked me stuck out and it was this: "Why did you ask me to put sickness on you?" I said, "Lord I did not…"

Before I could go further he placed images of the past into my head reminding me of those times I wished I was sick and would eventually die. I could not refute those moments. I then got a clear understanding that, we must not only be careful of the things we say and do, but also of the things we think.

He told me he was going to heal me and I remember when his healing power came a few weeks later. I felt intense heat and pressure on my back for about two hours – it was as if someone was standing on my back. And today I am totally healed and pain free without the intervention of medical surgery!

With that being said, I believe the opposite is quite the same. What if we learned how to use our imagination wisely – and think ourselves out of every dramatic or horrible situation we find ourselves in? Our words are powerful, but our thoughts have power too; so get your thought life together!

You can be rewarded by what you think. So until then – be careful what you think!

"You will keep in perfect peace all who trust in you, all whose thoughts are fixed on you!" Isaiah 26:3 (NLT)

Hope Writer: Author Terry-Ann Scott (Mandeville, Jamaica, West Indies)

Haitian Creole (English)
"Ou ap kenbe ak kè poze pafè tout moun ki mete konfyans yo nan ou, tout ki gen panse yo se fiks sou ou!" *Ezayi 26:3 (NLT)* **Hope Translator: Kirk Louis (Midwest City, Oklahoma, USA)**

91. Hope Artist Reflection: "Chosen Chains"

English (French)
Hope Artist: Jessica D. Mason
Location: Forest, Virginia, USA

I've done no wrong, have been proven true—but yet I choose to appeal to you.
I am not on trial though it seems;
I'm only a defense of the Risen King.
I witness to the fact of the God that you lack,
has found me and moved me from darkness to light.
His SON bore my shame, and took on God's wrath, and passed me his righteousness, in exchange for my rags.

My penalty—he paid—my charges are erased.
I'm free to go—but here's the thing—on my feet are chosen chains.
I know to stand before you talking of a LORD that adores you may sound strange.
Even so, to know the journey I made to you was laced in pain, but these are chosen chains you see—because of what Christ has done for me.
This is what he's called me to be—a prisoner of Grace—that the captives may be set free.
This is why I stand here clean, yet bound by chains you've been allowed to place on me; that one day your blinded

eyes may see... CHOSEN chains

What is the name of this piece of artwork?
"Chosen Chains"

What inspired you to create this piece of art?
It is a poem given to me by the Holy Spirit on November 5, 2013. It is in reference to Acts chapter 26.

How do you see hope within your artwork?
It is a picture of the freedom of a believer to choose to walk through binding circumstances and confining seasons to reach the lost for Jesus Christ.

What is one Christian scripture that is connected to your art?
Romans 8:28 says, "And we know that all things work together for good to those who love God, to those who are the called according to His purpose." (NKJV)

How does religion and culture influence your work?
We understand that it's because God loved us that he sent Jesus to set us free from the captivity of sin and eternal separation from God – and out of love for Christ we choose to trust God to walk us through those "all things work together," just so that He can get the glory and somebody can come to know the wonderful freedom of the Cross.

French (English)
Romains 8:28 dit, "Et nous savons que toutes choses concourent au bien de ceux qui aiment Dieu à ceux qui sont appelés selon son dessein." (NKJV) **Hope Translator: Erika Lobe**

(Baltimore, Maryland, USA)

92. Don't Only Praise God When The Sun Is Out

English (Swahili)

"Every good and perfect gift is from above, coming down from the Father of heavenly lights, who does not change like shifting shadows." James 1:17 (NIV)

Growing up attending church, I would always hear the phrase, "God is good all the time." And it's no wonder why this sentence is used so widely; God's eternal glory and steadfast nature are some of His many characteristics that instill hope within us and give us faith.

It is comforting to know that, in the midst of all of the ups and downs in this life, God will always be a faithful rock on which we can stand. Yet, if it is true that God is forever good, then why do we allow our emotions to determine how passionately we praise Him? Should our thanks not be the same when we're happy as when we're sad, angry, or lonely?

I recently realized that I praise God more eagerly when the sun is out. My mood is greatly affected by the weather, and so I'm much happier when the sun is shining. When I open my blinds to a bright and sunny morning, it is easy for me to take the time to pray to God, thanking Him for a new day. However, when it is overcast or raining, I find it harder to thank God with the same fervor.

That I allow my emotions and the weather to affect my praise to God illustrates an issue that I believe many

Christians face. Often, we let immediate, temporal situations blind our view of God's eternal greatness. We allow the rain, the trials in our lives, to keep us from praising God – and only when the sun is out, when things are going our way, do we thank God for what He has done for us.

However, it is important to remember that God is forever the same, and is therefore forever worthy of our praise. He always has great plans for us *(Jeremiah 29:11)*, and is always providing for us *(Matthew 6:26-34)*. God is the only constant in a world of temporary, and therefore we must remember to praise Him even when the sun isn't out.

Hope Writer: Niya Tanyi (Los Angeles, California, USA)

Swahili (English)
"Kila kipawa chema na kila zawadi kamilifu hutoka mbinguni, ikishuka kutoka kwa Baba wa nuru za mbinguni ambaye huwa habadiliki kama vivuli." Yakobo 1:17 *(NIV)* **Hope Translator: Merchades Method Rutechura (Dar es Salaam, Tanzania, East Africa)**

93. Thank God For The Body of Christ

English (Afrikaans)
So, God provided for me to stay in the Bay Area – getting a school psychologist's salary as well as the school district paying for a licensed psychologist to supervise me. But, if I am honest, sometimes I wish the door was opened to go to Washington, DC. This school year has been tough and I've already experienced burnout!

New changes in the school district caused a lot of chaos. I have to serve more kids in the same amount of time, we don't have permanent teachers for two of the classes at the school and we lost a staff position because the district thought we didn't need it.

On top of this, I was feeling very overwhelmed with the children's ministry that I direct. I was feeling under-appreciated in two big areas of my life: work and church.

I've cried many nights, I've had sleepless nights for almost two months now, and for the very first time in my life I uttered the words, "I think I am depressed." I've felt sad before, but never depressed.

But even in the midst of this depression, God showed me the true value of being in a Christian community. I cried in front of the other ministry members and they prayed for me and agreed to share the burdens I needed them to carry for the ministry. I cried on the phone to my mommy (yes, I still call her mommy) and she prayed for me. I cried on the phone to my auntie, and she prayed for me.

And I know that all of these people are still praying for me. Even in the midst of the sleeplessness nights, I know that God is there. Many friends reminded me that, even in the midst of feeling powerless, I have the Spirit of God, the same Spirit that raised Christ from the dead *(Romans 8:11)*.

Therefore, I can be raised from the feelings of depression back into life. Hallelujah! They also reminded me that no weapon formed against me shall prosper *(Isaiah 54:17)* and that I can cast all of my cares on Jesus *(1 Peter 5:7)* because He cares for me.

What a blessing to be comforted by Christ's community, to be able to be weak and allow my sisters and brothers to be strong for me. As a person who has to bear the burdens of youth on a daily basis, it is nice to know that I have people who can bear mine.

So I just encourage you, that when you are weak, God is strong. He is strong through the family of faith, our Christian brothers and sisters. Don't be afraid to call out for help when you need it. I'm not 100% better and I'm going through a process of growth and healing. I can count it all as joy because I know where my help comes from and I am alive today because of the Body of Christ!

"Two are better than one, because they have a good reward for their toil. For if they fall, one will lift up his fellow. But woe to him who is alone when he falls and has not another to lift him up!" Ecclesiastes 4:9-10 (ESV)

Hope Writer: Crystal Simmons (Oakland, California, USA)

Afrikaans (English)
"Twee is beter as een, want hulle het 'n goeie beloning vir hulle moeitevolle arbied". Prediker 4: 9 (Die Ganse Heilige Skrif Bible, 1940) **Hope Translator: Roxanne Van Wyk (Durban, South Africa)**

Trust

94. Trusting God With Your Path

English (German)

As strange as it may sound, I've written about my experience of transitioning to natural hair as God's way of preparing me for a time of trials and transition in my mind, heart and spirit. My hair became the channel God used to free me from low self-esteem and the need for acceptance so I could live in truth for Him. After clear revelation and accepting vulnerability, I changed my outward appearance with fear of what would happen next.

There were so many times when I was unsure of what to do with my hair and in my life, simultaneously. I found myself divorced before the age of 30, unemployed, lonely, misunderstood, confused, and with a head full of hair that I was unfamiliar with!

The revelation to go through this outward transformation was a God-inspired vision. All I knew was that God wanted to do something great in me through this experience. But I quickly learned that the frustrating part about vision is that the path and journey aren't always clear. I needed a clear plan for this transition. I needed to know how I would get to the other side which held promises of joy and fulfillment. But God wanted me to trust Him with the plan so that He could empower me to live the vision.

A scripture that encouraged me as I learned to trust God with my path is *Proverbs 3:5-6: "Trust God from the bottom of your heart; don't try to figure out everything on your own. Listen for God's voice in everything you do, everywhere you go; he's the one who will keep you on track." (MSG)*

As I endured all of the different "here we go again" moments in my life, I learned that it wasn't for me to figure out what to do. Each time I acknowledged this, an answer came, followed by peace. This was God's way of increasing my faith in Him and reassuring me that He has my best interest at heart.

The key for us is to accept God's love, develop a personal relationship and consistent communication with God, and believe that our paths and lives will lead us to God's purpose for us. As we develop our relationship with God through Jesus Christ, we remain focused on God's plan and not our fears.

Our fears cause us to lose sight of our hope in God. But when you are afraid, reflect on the love, grace, mercy and compassion of Christ – and let it be a reminder that you can trust Him with your path.

Hope Writer, Margaret A. Brunson (Raleigh, North Carolina, USA)

Malayalam (English)
"Poorna hridayathode Yehovayil asrayikkuka; Swntha vivekathil oonnaruthu. Ninte ella vazhikalilum avane ninachu kolka; avan ninte pathakale nereyakkum." Sadrishiya vakyangal 3:5-6 **Hope Translator: Gladson Thomas (Kottayam, Kerala, India)**

95. Trust and Obey

English (Jamaican Patois)
Four years ago, the Lord instructed me to give up all I had and go to Australia. In 2009, I left my job, gave away all

my possessions, and blindly obeyed. The savings I left Jamaica with ran out quickly, as the cost of living was way beyond anything I could imagine.

Although I believed when the Lord told me that he would "take care of me," I became frustrated. I searched for jobs but was unsuccessful and God remained silent when I inquired of Him. Discouragement came but I encouraged myself with the Word of God that said: *"Trust in the Lord with all your heart, and do not lean on your own understanding. In all your ways acknowledge him, and he will make straight your paths." Proverbs 3: 5-6 (NIV)*

About six weeks after my arrival – when I had resolved not to send out any more applications – I received a job. They needed someone with a combination of skills that I had. I subsequently received a two-year contract and led the project to successful completion in 2011.

My success in that job has eventually propelled me into the industry where I'm currently employed and being used of God to touch lives in the Western Pacific region. It is important to trust and obey the word of God, when he speaks, knowing that, *"If you are willing and obedient, You shall eat the good of the land." Isaiah 1:19 (NKJV)*

God doesn't always show you what's going to happen when He instructs you to "go!" What he requires is obedience. Today I encourage you, that, if God has asked you to do something that seems difficult, then trust him – as I'm confident that He will direct your path.

Hope Writer: Dr. Stephanie Fletcher (Sydney, New South Wales, Australia)

Jamaican Patois (English)

"If yu nuh hard ears and yu do wha yu suppose fi duh, den yu wi get fi nyaam all a di good food weh inna de lan and nuff good tings wi happen to yuh." Isaiah 1:19 (NKJV) **Hope Translator: Dr. Stephanie Fletcher (Sydney, New South Wales, Australia)**

96. Pilgrim Notes: Providence

English (French)

"So Abraham called that place, 'The Lord Will Provide'..." Gen. 22:14 (NIV)

In one of our best-loved hymns we sing, "I . . . was blind, but now I see."

This happened, literally, to me. My bicycle teammates and I were 12 months into a 13-month bicycle journey from Beijing to Paris. We were approaching our destination – the "City of Lights" – and I had an eye infection.

The glasses I had brought along had been accidentally left somewhere in Bulgaria at a lunch stop. All I had were contacts and some cheap prescription sunglasses. Our bicycle lifestyle was rugged and dirty; putting contact lenses in and out of my eyes had given me that eye infection. So I got by with my sunglasses by day, with a bit of a blurry haze at night.

I remember biking in a western German city after dark, still wearing the sunglasses – unable to make out shapes until they were quite close to me. I tried to stay close to my teammates' blinking rear light, and kept praying that I wouldn't smash into another biker or pedestrian. I wondered what I'd do when we biked to the Paris airport at 2 AM in several weeks, but thought perhaps by then it would be cleared up.

It was not.

In big cities on budget bicycle trips, you have to find a place to stay. It's nearly impossible to camp for free. One place, right at the end, seemed to be one of our only options. We were worried though, because the host said that the second night we'd be there, there was going to be a party. We just wanted a quiet place to stay, not some party house – but, being desperate, we took it.

Our first good portent happened as we were trying to navigate the streets of Paris and find the address we'd been given. As we were discussing where to go on a busy street corner, a young man came up to us and asked if we needed help.

We showed him the address we were looking for, and he said, "Oh, you must be the world travelers. That's my best friend Julien's place. He is hosting my wedding reception tomorrow night, and you are most welcome. I will take you there."

Julien was our second good portent. He was charming, kind, and generous. He had a marvelous flat where we could fit our stuff and be comfortable, and still not interfere with the party prep. He also noticed I had an eye infection.

"Here," he said, "I have some disinfectant. Also, what is your prescription?" I told him, and he said, "That was my prescription until two months ago, when I had Lasik surgery to correct my vision. You can have my old pair of glasses if you like."

Of all the people in all the neighborhoods of Paris, we met up with Julien and his friend, who helped us along our journey by guiding us to a place and helping a "blind" man see. The party was refined and elegant – with desserts, fruit, wine, and all sorts of French cheeses. The glasses worked just fine, and I could see clearly on our 2 AM ride to the airport later that week.

I continued to wear those glasses for several weeks, until I could get an eye exam and another pair of my own back in the United States.

I am grateful that the Lord we serve, who is both the God of Abraham and Jesus Christ, still opens the eyes of the blind and provides for those in need.

Hope Writer: Andrew Spidahl (Holland, Michigan, USA)

French (English)
"Abraham donna à ce lieu:« Le Seigneur pourvoira." Genèse 22:14 **Hope Translator: Andrew Spidahl (Holland, Michigan, USA)**

97. Protector God

English (Xhosa)
I once had a vision where I was standing on a sandy beach. My only way forward was through a passage too narrow, which ran between two solid walls of wet rock higher and longer than the eye could see. I was asked if I could make

the walls come down.

I touched the rock, but knew without trying that this was something that I could never do with my own two hands. It was suggested that I try asking for help. I did, and a man in full armor appeared. The man raised his scepter and as he waved it back and forth, he erased the walls with ease. I was left looking out at the ocean and its vast peace.

I remember being refreshed that day with how easy it was to ask for help, how quickly the man came and how simply he erased something that was, for me, impossible.

We build walls without knowing. We build them for protection and out of fear. While we are fortifying our heart from the bad, we can seal it so tight that even God begins to find it harder and harder to enter in. We continually seek God's face, but without letting down our walls, He too is left peering through the gates.

God is asking us to let down our guard, to walk with Him and to trust Him to protect us; for what fortress could be greater than the God Almighty Himself?

"You are my strength, I sing praise to you; you, God are my fortress, my God whom I can rely." Psalm 59:17 (NIV)

We can learn in this world, to rely on ourselves and to trust no one. But the word tells us, *"Do not be afraid or terrified because of them, for the Lord your God goes with you; he will never leave you nor forsake you." Deuteronomy 31:6 (NIV)*

God wants you to rely on Him. By trying to heal from the outside in, building protection before surrendering what is deepest, the fortress can begin to suffocate you. Yes, it may keep the bad out; but the walls have also blocked out the beauty that God has waiting.

I invite you, brothers and sisters, to examine your man-made walls. You may have built them, but God will do the demolition freely, replace them with His authority and shower you with peace. *"Those who trust in the Lord will find new strength."* Isaiah 40:31 (NLT)

Hope Writer: Sonya Taly (Providence, Rhode Island, USA)

Xhosa (English)
"Mandla am, ndiya kukubethela uhadi; Ngokuba uThixo yingxonde yam, nguThixo wam onenceba." Psalm 59:17 **Hope Translator: Sivu Tywabi (Johannesburg, South Africa)**

98. One Little Word

English (Sepedi)
Hope Artist: Rod Spidahl
Location: Fergus Falls, Minnesota, USA

"One Little Word"

Fears—
as verbal, noun,
or adjective.

Appearing
in so many forms—
and don't forget
all the relatives.

But who cares,
these literary bounds
when in the night
they burst their bonds,
come leaping on,
a'ganging, a'hunting
and all-ranging
as famished demons?

But if we bring
and increase them,
become or release them,
surely words matter
now
when I must speak
the Name above all names
that will defeat them.

What is the name of this piece of artwork?
"One Little Word"

What inspired you to create this piece of art?
In the late, late night and early mornings, between waking and sleeping, fears I only read about – or thought were the stuff of movie and story – can afflict me. Experience has taught me that I do not have to figure things out but can, as the Gospel stories remind me, simply speak the Name of Jesus against the dark storm. Martin Luther's hymn, "A Mighty Fortress" has the line, "One little Word shall fell him (Satan)."

How do you see hope within your artwork?
I have learned to name and admit my weaknesses, afflictions, sufferings, trials, and, yes, fears and anxieties.

Hope lies in being transparent to God and, when appropriate, to trusted friends, because confessing the truth of our frailty and struggles is the door that opens to God's provision. Hope lies in gut-wrenching honesty.

What is one Christian scripture that is connected to your art?

"That is why, for Christ's sake, I delight in weaknesses, in insults, in hardships, in persecutions, in difficulties. For when I am weak, then I am strong." 2 Corinthians 12:10 (NIV)

How do religion and culture influence your work?

Being part of a culture that uses fear, suspense, and violence for entertaining us, we often think that what we read or watch is neutral or will not affect us. Cultures are value-driven in various ways, and therefore, the line we sometimes like to draw between culture and religion is often not there.

Religion consists of those things that we find to be uniquely real and those values we use to stimulate our senses and move us to action and long-term choices. Religion and culture can both use fear to motivate instead of forgiveness and love. What we should ask about our use of culture or religion is if, in the end, what we use to give us our value really has the power to free us from fear and hypocrisy and become more fully human.

Sepedi (English)

"Ke ka fao, bakeng sa Kriste. Ke kgotsofatšwago ke go rwala mafokodi le mahlapa, le maima le dihlomaro ka gare ga mathata. Gobane ge ke fokola, ke mo ke nago le maatla." 2 Bakorinte 12:10 (NIV) **Hope Translator: Warrel Stephen Mothoa (Soweto, South Africa)**

99. The Process of Obeying Involves Questions

English (German)
In praying about which testimony I should write about, I decided to write about what God is taking me through right now. I finished my doctorate about a year ago and God blessed me with a job that I liked – and was helping me reach my next goal in life as a licensed psychologist.

But, in prayer, I heard God tell me that I had to leave my job. I was like, "For real? How can God ask me to leave a job that was helping me towards my goal?" Moreover, my only other option was to get an internship that paid considerably less money, with no health benefits!

Besides, I was sure that the job that I had now was what God had promised me. I'd been working at this job since graduate school; I loved my boss; my coworkers were great. I was doing exactly what I wanted to do.

So I wrestled with what I heard. Was it really God telling me this? God answered yes. I asked, "Will I be able to get another job? Am I good enough to compete?" I didn't believe that I could get another job, especially in this economy.

Yes, I have a doctorate, but I didn't think that I had the skills to compete for an internship. When I applied for them, it seemed as if my answers to those questions were confirmed. I didn't get any of the internships. And so I was left asking myself, "What is going on? God told me to leave, but God has not provided. What am I to do?" Well, I kept applying!

My pastor preached a sermon, while I was trying to figure

out what God wanted. He preached on the story of Abraham and Isaac in *Genesis 22*. In short, God asked Abraham to sacrifice his only son Isaac – a son that was a promise from God, given to him in his old age – and who was supposed to carry the family line.

Just when Abraham was about to kill Isaac, the angel of the Lord told him to stop. At this point God knew that Abraham feared Him – and provided a ram for Abraham to sacrifice to him instead of Isaac.

God spoke to me that day, and showed me that the job He gave to me was a promise. I believe that He wanted to see how much I trusted Him. Would I be willing to give up what He promised to me to obey Him?

Shortly after, I was blessed with an extra day-and-a-half at my job, receiving more pay and more hours towards reaching my goal as a licensed psychologist!

But the biggest blessing was going through the process of obeying what God told me. It really challenged me to ask myself, "Where does my security lie? Am I willing to go when God wants me to go? Who do I really trust, God or my abilities?"

I'm grateful that God provided more pay and work, but I'm even more grateful for the questions that came up. The questions came so that I may know God more and cultivate a deeper relationship with Him. The questions came to challenge me in my level of trust towards Him. I now know better what it means to trust.

"Those who know your name will trust in you, for you, LORD,

have never forsaken those who seek you." *—Psalm 9:10 (NIV)*

Hope Writer: Crystal Simmons (Oakland, California, USA)

German (English)
"Darum vertraut dir, wer deinen Namen kennt; denn du, Herr, verlässt keinen, der dich sucht." Psalm 9,10 *(NIV)* **Hope Translator: Ha Feh (Kiel, Germany)**

100. A Father's Promise

English (Filipino)
It always amazes me when I am put in situations that reveal characteristics of God, the Father – mainly because I don't currently have biological children. And even though I have a great relationship with my earthly dad, it blows my mind when God shows how good of a Father He really is.

So here's how the story goes: I took a trip down to East Texas visiting my family when I, my oldest brother and his son decided to take a trip to the local grocery store. The crisp wind complemented the warm kiss of the bright sun – the perfect summer day. As we entered the store, engaged in conversation, my nephew interrupts to ask his father an often-dreaded question – by some parents. Apparently, my nephew didn't get the memo.

Childhood flashback: "Now when we get in here, don't ask for nothing!" says my stern-faced mother as we approach my favorite store. I remember thinking, "I only want a Matchbox car."

But when my wise young nephew approaches his father with this question, I was taken aback by the way he worded his request. You can already deduce that he is about to ask for something for his dad to purchase. This is true. So he begins with, "Daddy? Do you remember you told me that you were going to buy me that game?" "Yea," replies his dad. "Can I get it now?" "Yea, Son," says his dad without hesitation.

My nephew understands the meaning of his father's promise. Had he asked for something that he had not been promised, he probably would have gotten declined, but since what he was asking for lined up with what his dad had already obligated, he found himself with a granted request.

When it comes to God, the Father, he is ready, willing and more than able to fulfill every promise that He's made to us in His word! No request too great or small. God isn't afraid of the big requests. As a matter of fact, he welcomes them. He knows exactly what you can handle based on your stewardship.

So I welcome you to search God's word today, and most importantly commune with Him regularly. In your relationship, you'll find hidden tokens and priceless promises that He so generously lavishes upon His own children.

"And this same God who takes care of me will supply all your needs from his glorious riches, which have been given to us in Christ Jesus." Philippians 4:19 (NLT)

Hope Writer: Zamansky L. Moore (Houston, Texas, USA)

Filipino (English)
"At pupunan ng aking Dios ang bawa't kailangan ninyo ayon sa kaniyang mga kayamanan sa kaluwalhatian kay Cristo Jesus."
Mga Taga Filipos 4:19 (NLT) **Hope Translator: Rose Renie Canlas (Baguio City, Philippines)**

101. Facing Fear and Overcoming the STORM with God

English (Swahili)
A month ago I went back to the island of St. Kitts, which I had not visited in 5-and-a-half years. I'd been serving as a Community Development Worker as a US Peace Corps Volunteer – before I was assaulted, strangled, robbed, and had an attempted rape on my body, mind, and spirit.

Four years ago I went through a trial that sent my attacker to prison for 46 years. Since then I have worked to heal from Post-Traumatic Stress Disorder, nightmares, anxiety, and fear.

My trip to St. Kitts was a big deal. I'd had many positive experiences serving there, but my last encounter had been so traumatic and painful. I thought I was there primarily to have the courage to visit and confront the man who'd assaulted me, which did not happen. God knows!

I remember sitting in the home of my adopted family. On the local TV station they were showing a celebration for the prisoners. People in the community were watching that party for them – with a live band, food, music – the whole works.

Yes, some could watch their imprisoned loved ones. But,

what about those people whose perpetrators were in that same prison? How did we – as victims and survivors – feel? Did we want to see our rapists, attackers, and robbers? It was only television, but my heart raced.

What if I saw the man who'd hurt me? It had been years since I'd had an anxiety attack. I took a deep breath. Before I left the room, I asked my adopted sister, "Could you please turn the station? The man who assaulted me is in that prison." She quickly changed the channel and noted, "You should have told me." Deep breath!

My trip to St. Kitts ultimately became one of the most restorative experiences of my life. I revisited every place that had brought me peace at one point, but had brought me fear at another point. I visited all of the girls I had taught and who had taught me. They were now working women!

I went to the churches at which I had once taught and preached. I reconnected with those churches, teaching and preaching again! I walked down the deserted path where I had once seen my attacker's face. Instead, I now saw the sun, palm trees, and small monkeys!

I walked around the community – and instead of being afraid, I received hugs and cheek kisses from friends. Though I was afraid to walk alone at night, I slept peacefully. No nightmares, no pain, and when anxiety came up I took a deep breath, said a prayer, and talked to God.

Healing is a journey. Sometimes it is a battle to get to the other side of a storm. But it's possible. With God all things are possible!

I encourage anyone reading *101 Testimonies of Hope* to never give up on your healing. Never give up on your hope, never give up on God, never give up on yourself. God does love you – and your situation can get better.

Years ago my aunt told me to keep this scripture close. She was right.

Psalms 91:1-4 (NKJV) reads:

"He who dwells in the secret place of the Most High Shall abide under the shadow of the Almighty. I will say of the LORD, 'He is my refuge and my fortress; My God, in Him I will trust.' Surely He shall deliver you from the snare of the fowler And from the perilous pestilence. He shall cover you with His feathers, And under His wings you shall take refuge; His truth shall be your shield and buckler."

Amen.

Argrow "Kit" Evans (Rock Island, Illinois, USA)
Founder, Testimonies of Hope:
The Intercultural Christian Devotional Website

Swahili (English)
Zaburi 91:1-4 (NKJV) inasomeka: Aketiye mahali pa siri pa Mungu Mkuu atakaa katika kivuli cha Mungu Mwenye Nguvu. Nitamwambia BWANA, "Wewe ni kimbilio langu na ngome yangu; Mungu wangu, ninayekutumainia." Hakika Mungu atakuokoa katika mtego; atakukinga na maradhi mabaya. Atakufunika kwa manyoya yake, na chini ya mabawa yake utapata usalama wake; Uaminifu wake utakulinda na kukukinga. **Hope Translator: Merchades Method Rutechura (Dar es Salaam, Tanzania, East Africa)**

OUR VISION

Testimonies of Hope

Together, Christians in intentional online community from around the world will share testimonies, faith-based art, and witness about suffering, healing, and restoration to encourage each other and nurture hope. This will help foster and strengthen the unwavering hope that comes from being in community and having a relationship with Jesus Christ.

"Let us hold fast to the confession of our hope without wavering, for he who has promised is faithul. And let us consider how to provoke one another to love and good deeds, not neglecting to meet together, as is the habit of some, but encouraging one another, and all the more as you see the Day approaching." Hebrews 10: 23-25 (NRSV)

ABOUT THE FOUNDER
ARGROW "KIT" EVANS

National trainer, speaker, and activist with Pace e Bene Nonviolence Service and the National Association of Students Against Violence Everywhere, Argrow "Kit" Evans is woman who is passionate about God, nonviolence, hope, and serving others. She has been a trainer and activist for many years working relentlessly in the areas of conflict resolution, nonviolence education, violence prevention, and assisting people in healing from violence and abuse.

Kit holds a BA in Communications Studies (UNC Chapel Hill), an MA in Teaching: Special Education (Trinity Washington University), an MA in Social Justice and Community Development (SIT Graduate Institute), and an MDiv degree (Pacific School of Religion). She is a Teacher For America and US Peace Corps Alumni. She has studied worked, and served in England, Japan, South Africa, Tanzania, Kenya, Saint Lucia, Saint Kitts and Nevis.

In May of 2008, Kit became a survivor of an extremely violent crime. After surviving the attack, she became more driven to promote the power of nonviolent social change and spreading hope.

Kit is the founder of Testimonies of Hope: The Intercultural Christian Devotional Website (www.testimoniesofhope.org). She now uses her education, teachings on nonviolence and conflict resolution, travels, experiences with dance, healing, and spirituality as a speaker, life coach, teacher, and activist (www.kitevanslive.com). Kit resides in Rock Island, Illinois, USA.

61898172R00136